To Dad + Gisela's friends
Marilyn + Darrell Hall.

Jeff Mechstutt

D1262491

Win the
ermuda Bowl
~With Me

Jeff Meckstroth
Marc Smith

MASTER POINT PRESS · TORONTO

Master Point Press
331 Douglas Ave.
Toronto, Ontario, Canada
M5M 1H2

(416) 781-0351
www.masterpointpress.com

Distributed in the USA by Barricade Books
Suite 308a, 185 Bridge Plaza North
Fort Lee, NJ, 07024

(800) 59-BOOKS

Canadian Cataloguing in Publication Data

Meckstroth, Jeff 1956-
Win the bermuda bowl with me

ISBN 1-894154-33-9

I. Bermuda Bowl, 2. Contract bridge — Tournaments — Bermuda.
I. Smith, Marc, 1960- .II. Title.

GV 1282. 62. B47M42 2001   794.41'58   C00-933102-6

Cover and Interior design: Olena S. Sullivan
Editor: Ray Lee
Interior format and copyediting: Deanna Bourassa

Printed and bound in Canada by Webcom Limited

1 2 3 4 5 6 7   07 06 05 04 03 02 01

Foreword

Jeff and I have been playing bridge together for more than a quarter of a century. In that time, we have discussed thousands of auctions and developed our own theories on how to react to most bidding situations. In this book, Jeff outlines many of the ideas that we have adopted over the years. He also offers numerous insights into our bidding philosophy, although thankfully, the book was not long enough for him to give away all of our secrets. Seriously, though, while you may not always agree with Jeff's views, they have stood us in good stead through a great many victories. I hope you find them both interesting and helpful.

In our years as a partnership, I have been privileged to watch Jeff handle the dummy with incredible skill. His declarer play is as good as that of anyone who has ever played the game. In this book, he explains his thinking on each deal, from his reaction on first seeing dummy through the making of his initial plan and how he adjusts his thinking as the play develops.

The deals here were all played against top quality opposition at the highest level — in the Bermuda Bowl itself. I hope you will find Jeff's observations on the pressures of playing in the world's greatest bridge event interesting. Reading through the manuscript brought back many memories for me — how close we came to missing the cut in the Round Robin at the 1995 Bermuda Bowl and the exciting quarter-final match in Bermuda 2000 are two examples that spring to mind. I also remember many of the deals, and between them the authors have done a wonderful job of recreating the tense atmosphere in which they occurred.

Eric Rodwell

PHOTO CREDITS

CONTENTS

Foreword   5

Introduction   9

The Round Robin   13

Match 1	*Poland*	*16*
Match 2	*New Zealand*	*20*
Match 3	*Great Britain*	*20*
Match 4	*Canada*	*27*
Match 5	*Sweden*	*28*
Match 6	*Norway*	*31*
Match 7	*Italy*	*33*
Match 8	*Poland*	*37*
Match 9	*New Zealand*	*38*
Match 10	*Great Britain*	*42*
Match 11	*Canada*	*47*
Match 12	*Sweden*	*48*
Match 13	*Norway*	*49*
Match 14	*Italy*	*53*

The Quarter-final   63

The Semifinal   101

The Final   139

INTRODUCTION

To any bridge player, the Bermuda Bowl is *the* world championship — the one title above all that is symbolic of world bridge supremacy. As of the time this book is first available, Jeff Meckstroth has participated in six Bermuda Bowls, each at a different venue, and has won four of them. The Bermuda Bowl competition described in these pages is not, in fact, any one of these events, but a fictitious championship made up from deals actually played by Jeff during his twenty years experience of the Bermuda Bowl. In most cases, the real-life opponents were those named in this book, although there are some exceptions. In the chapters describing the knockout stages we had to choose a single opponent for each round in this mythical championship, whereas Jeff has actually played, for example, four finals against four different countries. Jeff chose to stage this 'amalgamation' in Beijing, which is his favorite of the six venues.

If you are expecting to find in these pages a series of hands in which Jeff Meckstroth brings home ambitious contracts on esoteric squeezes, you will be disappointed. The problems on the deals included here are very similar to those you are likely to face when you next sit down to play. The difference is that, while reading these hands, you will have the benefit of listening to one of the world's truly great players explain his thought processes. Why should you switch to a diamond rather than a spade? Why should you play for a 3-3 break rather than take a finesse? What difference does it make to lead a diamond early? What are the clues that should point you to the winning line of play or defense? Jeff's explanations help to answer these and many other common questions.

Eric Rodwell and Jeff Meckstroth are widely acknowledged as the best partnership bidders ever to have played the game. Does that mean that you are going to see dozens of twenty-bid sequences as they wend their way to a slam on some delicate 4-3 fit? Not at all — the type of bidding problem addressed here is no different from those you face at the table every time you play. Should you overcall or double? When and how high should you preempt? Should you sacrifice? Should you double? To help you to understand why one option will work more often than another, Jeff explains the reasoning that led him to choose a particular action when he held the hand. We will even see a couple of situations in which Eric and Jeff have a misunderstanding; they have now discussed those auctions so that the problem will never recur. Perhaps these are situations that you should ask your regular partner about too. You may be surprised to find that you are on different wavelengths.

You will hear Jeff's views on a wide range of common bidding situations and everyone reading this book, from beginner to World Champion, will pick up some tips from the master. In addition to the tips on bidding, play and defense, Jeff also provides some amusing stories about some of his opponents. He offers us a rare insight into the psychological aspect of playing under pressure, in the spotlight of a World Championship.

Most of the text of this book is written in the first person plural. The "We" and "Our" in the narrative (as in "We pick up...", "This is our hand...", "What shall we do now..." etc.) should be read as meaning "Jeff and the reader". This enables him to discuss his thinking with you directly as the hand is progressing. The odd notes that appear in a different type and use "I" as the pronoun explain what Jeff actually did at the table and move the hand on to the next stage. This format is also used to introduce the various opponents. We've included pictures of Jeff's opponents, and also of many of his teammates in world competition, especially those who have formed part of the formidable Nickell team.

We hope you enjoy playing the hands in this book, for that is exactly what you will be doing. We wish you luck as you set off to play in your first Bermuda Bowl.

Win the
Bermuda Bowl
With Me

The Round Robin

I have been looking forward to this Bermuda Bowl for some time. China has always been high on the list of places I wanted to visit, and playing a World Championship in Beijing will be quite an experience. I am looking forward to visiting Tiananmen Square and the Great Hall of the People. With luck, we'll also have the time to travel out to see the Great Wall.

My wife, Shirlee, and I set off a full week before the championships are due to begin. We stop over for a few days in Hong Kong, in part to get adjusted to the time change but also to get into a relaxed frame of mind before the serious business gets under way. Then it's onwards to Beijing to join up with my teammates and catch up with the many old friends who will be there. We arrive at Capital International Airport, located some twenty miles northeast of the city. We are met at the gate and whisked away to the venue, the magnificent Continental Grand Hotel, a seventeen-story palace situated in the Asian Games Village. I had expected to be surrounded by historical sites but this region of Beijing, including the hotel, was built in 1990 for the Asian games and it is ultra-modern.

The hotel is huge, with six different restaurants, a host of private VIP dining rooms and more than 1200 rooms. There are even two karaoke bars — I wonder idly if I will find myself singing some familiar ballad with backing from the likes of Helgemo, Robson and Soloway before the event finishes. I hope not, but it wouldn't surprise me!

It's worth mentioning here the overall atmosphere of these events, as it would probably surprise people who have never attended a World Championship. It's all strictly business during the day when play is in progress but, unlike events at home, the bridge finishes in the early evening and then things get very social. The bar gets busy and everyone enjoys a few beers. Most teams go for an excellent meal, often in large groups comprising a couple of teams plus their wives and/or friends. Then it's back to business again the next morning and we do it all over again.

I meet up with Eric, who arrived yesterday, and together we go to check out the playing areas. Conditions are superb — plenty of space, good lighting and not too hot.

The draw for the Round Robin is tough but we knew it would be. In principle, these are the best sixteen teams in the world. The field is divided into two pools of eight. We will play a double Round Robin of 20-board matches over five days, with four teams from each pool surviving to the knockout stage. The other teams in our group are Italy, Poland, Norway, Sweden, Great Britain, Canada and New Zealand. Of those, only the New Zealanders would be considered to have little chance of qualifying and then only because they are something of an unknown quantity. Not that the other group is much easier — it contains the other USA team, Brazil, France, Pakistan, Indonesia and the hosts, China, along with outsiders Australia and South Africa.

The key to surviving the Round Robin comfortably is to crush the weakest teams. Doing so gives you a margin for error against the stronger teams. Ideally, you also want to win your group, rather than just simply qualifying. Winning gives you the choice of opponents in the knockout stage, which can be a major advantage as there is a carry-forward if you play a team you have met earlier in the event.

We open against Poland. We are to be featured on Vugraph but that will not faze any of the players involved in this match. All are experienced campaigners at this level. Eric leads the way into the Open Room… **are you ready to take your seat?**

DAY ONE

Match 1 vs. Poland

The Poles are all good guys. It often seems remarkable how similar all of their pairs are — they all play Polish Club and they are all extremely tough opponents: aggressive bidders and excellent card players. This particular Polish team includes the four Poles I know best — Cezary Balicki, Adam Zmudzinski, Marek Szymanowski and Marcin Lesniewski. I've spent many enjoyable evenings playing blackjack with these guys in casinos around the world.

The match is fairly flat in our room but the final deal looks to have potential for a swing. With both sides vulnerable, our hand is:

$$\spadesuit — \quad \heartsuit\ A\,K\,J\,10\,8\,5\,3 \quad \diamondsuit\ Q\,J\,9 \quad \clubsuit\ A\,Q\,5$$

We are playing a Strong Club system so we have no problem here — **one club**. Balicki, on our left, overcalls **one spade** and partner bids a natural and positive **one notrump**, promising a spade stopper. As we are in a game-forcing auction, we could bid a simple Two Hearts, but that covers a wide range of hands. Our philosophy is to let partner know we hold a real monster if possible and we can do so here without using too much space — by jumping to **three hearts**. This shows a very strong, one-suited hand with at least a semi-solid suit — something like a game-forcing Two Clubs opening in Standard.

Partner raises us to **four hearts**. **Are you tempted to bid on?**

You should not be — Four Hearts is the weakest bid he had available. With a suitable hand, he would cuebid one of the minors. His initial One Notrump told us that he has spade values and his failure to make a positive move over Three Hearts suggests he will have little else. Indeed, Four Hearts might not be a walk in the park...

WEST	NORTH	EAST	SOUTH
Balicki	*Eric*	*Zmudzinski*	*Us*
			1♣[1]
1♠	1NT	pass	3♡
pass	4♡	all pass	

1. Artifical, 16+.

West leads the six of spades and dummy appears with:

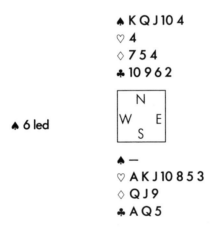

♠ K Q J 10 4
♡ 4
◇ 7 5 4
♣ 10 9 6 2

♠ 6 led

♠ —
♡ A K J 10 8 5 3
◇ Q J 9
♣ A Q 5

Dummy's king wins Trick 1 and we dispose of the low club. That can't be a bad start. We are unlikely to reach dummy again so we must choose which finesse to take. **Any ideas?**

After the unusual low spade lead, presumably away from the ace, we can place West with a tough hand to lead from — very likely, he has an honor in each suit. If this reasoning is correct, there is no point in finessing in either clubs or hearts. Our best chance seems to be to find the ten of diamonds onside.

Cezary Balicki

We therefore lead a low diamond and put in the nine, but that doesn't seem to have worked either — West wins the trick with the ten of diamonds. Balicki continues with the ace of diamonds and a third round of the suit to his partner's king. Zmudzinski then plays a club. What do you make of this?

There is one thing of which we can be certain — East does not hold the king of clubs. He would hardly give us a chance to take a winning finesse that we clearly cannot take for ourselves.

We go up with the ace of clubs and the king falls from West. When we cash the ace-king of hearts, West's queen comes down doubleton and we can claim our contract. Hmmm... It seems that playing on diamonds was the winning line of play after all. Taking a losing finesse in either clubs or hearts would still have left us with three inescapable diamond losers.

This was the full deal:

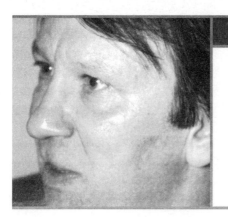

Marcin Lesniewski

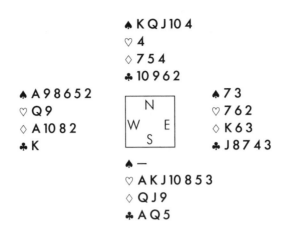

```
                 ♠ K Q J 10 4
                 ♡ 4
                 ◇ 7 5 4
                 ♣ 10 9 6 2
♠ A 9 8 6 5 2         ┌─────────┐         ♠ 7 3
♡ Q 9                 │    N    │         ♡ 7 6 2
◇ A 10 8 2            │ W     E │         ◇ K 6 3
♣ K                   │    S    │         ♣ J 8 7 4 3
                      └─────────┘
                 ♠ —
                 ♡ A K J 10 8 5 3
                 ◇ Q J 9
                 ♣ A Q 5
```

A game swing for us? Not at all. At the other table, our West avoided the low spade lead, choosing the ace instead! Declarer ruffed, laid down the top trumps felling the queen and drew East's last trump. Declarer then led the queen of diamonds, ducked to East's king. A diamond return would have left declarer with no chance but East chose to play a club and declarer played low. West won with the king but now found himself endplayed in a rather unusual fashion — a diamond lead gives away a trick in that suit and a spade allows declarer to pitch his diamonds on dummy's winners. Just another dull flat board!

We win the match but only just, by 3 IMPs, which translates into 16-14 in Victory Points. Still, it's better than a 3-IMP loss.

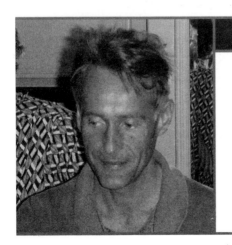

Adam Żmudziński

Match 2 vs. New Zealand

Eric and I sit out this match. The plan is that by the end of the first day all three of our pairs will have played twice and, we hope, everyone will be in some kind of groove.

As the New Zealanders were perceived as the weakest team, we are hopeful of scoring a large win but things don't go as planned. Not that our pairs play poorly — the opponents play fairly well and have one spectacular success with their unusual system.

We manage to win but only by 32-22, which is 17-13 in VPs.

Match 3 vs. Great Britain

We always seem to get drawn in the same group as Great Britain so we know most of their top pairs well. This is particularly true of Tony (Forrester) and Andrew (Robson), the British pair at our table for this match. We have played against them in the 'Naturalist vs Scientists' match in London, in the 'USA vs Europe' match in Italy, in numerous Macallans and Cap Geminis and in many US Nationals.

They are both really nice guys and great players. I consider them friends. Both have a good sense of humor, a quality I think is important for bridge — the ability to laugh helps one to relax at the table and it's much easier to concentrate when one is relaxed.

Despite both being great players, I have always felt that as a partnership they failed to bring out the best in each other. Why, I don't know. That's just my feeling. Getting the best out of both yourself and your partner is just one of many important factors for success at this game.

Nowadays one more often sees them on the same team but not in partnership and that seems to be working very well for them.

The match starts with what looks like a flat game for each side and then, vulnerable against not, we pick up this hand:

♠ K J 6   ♡ Q 10 8 6   ◇ 4   ♣ K J 9 6 2

East, Forrester, on our right, deals and passes. As anyone who has played regularly against us will know, we like to open whenever possible. But this hand is the wrong shape because we do not have a natural club opening at the one-level available. We therefore pass for now.

West opens with a 14-16 **one notrump** and, after two passes, it's up to us. Our options are either Pass or a systemic Two Clubs, showing clubs and a major. **Do you think we should bid?**

Our style is to bid over 1NT with decent hands that have some shape. This is certainly true if we have at least one major because, if we do have a game on, it is most likely to be in a major. Another good tactical reason for bidding on this particular hand is that partner is most likely to lead a diamond against 1NT and that doesn't rate to be good for us. We therefore back in with **two clubs** — clubs and a major.

You no doubt thought this was going to be a partscore battle, but you can throw that notion out of the window. The auction suddenly takes off. Robson jumps to **three diamonds** and Eric cuebids, **four diamonds**, asking us to bid our major. We oblige with **four hearts**. Thankfully, the auction ends without a double. Not that we should be surprised to find ourselves at the four-level. After all, this is what IMPs is all about — bidding and making games.

This has been the eventful auction:

WEST	NORTH	EAST	SOUTH
Robson	Eric	Forrester	Us
		pass	pass
1NT	pass	pass	2♣[1]
3◇	4◇[2]	pass	4♡
all pass			

1. Clubs and a major.
2. Please bid your major.

Andrew kicks off with the ace of diamonds and we can see:

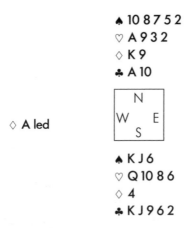

```
            ♠ 10 8 7 5 2
            ♡ A 9 3 2
            ◇ K 9
            ♣ A 10
                  ┌─────┐
                  │  N  │
  ◇ A led        │W   E│
                  │  S  │
                  └─────┘
            ♠ K J 6
            ♡ Q 10 8 6
            ◇ 4
            ♣ K J 9 6 2
```

The ace of diamonds lead is followed by a second diamond to dummy's king, on which we pitch a spade from hand. **How would you plan to amass ten tricks?**

We will not be able to cope with any nasty breaks but things are far from hopeless. There is nowhere to put our second spade so, if there are two spade losers, we will need a miracle in the trump suit. It therefore seems right to find out about spades before we do anything else, so let's play a spade next. East plays low and it's a clear favorite to play the notrump opener for the ace rather than the queen, so we put in the jack. West wins with the ace and returns a second spade to our king. That's the first hurdle overcome. **What next?**

It's still not clear how to play the trumps. Testing the clubs first may give us a clue. Thinking back to the bidding, we can see that doing so is not as dangerous as it might appear at first glance. West surely has six diamonds (for his jump to the three-level). He has already shown up with two spades and presumably also has at least two hearts. (East would probably have doubled with four hearts.) If this reasoning is correct, West cannot hold four clubs and thus the risk of East overruffing the third round is negligible.

We safely cash two top clubs and negotiate a club ruff in dummy, both defenders following, West with the queen on the third round.

What do we know about the defenders' hands? West has six diamonds and three clubs. Presumably, therefore, he began with a doubleton in each major. He surely would not have opened a 14-16 notrump with ♠Ax ♡Kx ◇AQJxxx ♣Qxx. With such playing strength, the risk of missing game would be far too high. No, surely East holds the king of hearts.

We cash the ace of hearts and play a second round towards our queen. East started with ♡KJx so the defenders make only one trump to go with their two aces. Ten tricks — plus 620.

At the other table, our East-West teammates buy the contract in a rather inelegant Four Diamonds. Fortunately, no one doubles. The contract drifts three off for -150 and 10 IMPs come our way.

After three more uninteresting deals, our hand with both sides vulnerable is:

♠ K 6   ♡ K   ◇ A J 10 9 8   ♣ A J 7 6 3

RHO passes and we must decide on an opening bid. The choices in our system are a strong One Club or a nebulous One Diamond, which is our catch-all opening — 10-15 HCP with at least two diamonds and a hand that cannot be opened with anything else. (A Two Clubs opening bid promises at least a six-card suit in our methods.)

Our Strong Club opening has a lower end of only 16 HCP so that is an easy choice on this hand — **one club**. There is also an important principle of bidding in which I believe strongly: if, early in the auction, one must either overbid a bit or underbid a bit, always choose the overbid. This will eliminate all future bidding problems as you will have already 'done justice' to expressing your values. I am sure this will be a recurring theme throughout this book.

Eric responds **two diamonds**, an artificial bid showing a balanced hand with 8-10 HCP. This is a distinct improvement on the standard Precision-style One Notrump response to show minimum balanced hands, as it allows the stronger hand to declare a notrump contract. This hand is a good example as we clearly want the lead coming up to our major-suit holdings, rather than through them.

We could bid one of our minor suits now but an eleven-trick game seems a long way off with this hand facing 8-10 balanced. The most likely game, if any game is making, must be in notrump, so let's bid it now — **three notrump**. The brief and uninformative auction has been:

WEST	NORTH	EAST	SOUTH
Robson	*Eric*	*Forrester*	*Us*
		pass	1♣[1]
pass	2♦[2]	pass	3NT
all pass			

1.   Artificial 16+
2.   Balanced, 8-10 HCP

Andrew leads the five of hearts and Eric produces:

```
              ♠ Q J 5 3
              ♡ 9 6 3 2
              ◇ Q 6 5
              ♣ K 9
              ┌─────────┐
              │    N    │
  ♡ 5 led     │ W     E │
              │    S    │
              └─────────┘
              ♠ K 6
              ♡ K
              ◇ A J 10 9 8
              ♣ A J 7 6 3
```

East plays the ten and our king of hearts wins Trick 1. We are still in the race. One option is to cross to the king of clubs and lead the queen of diamonds for a finesse. That doesn't seem like a high probability line of play though — in addition to the diamond finesse, we will also have to decide later whether to play for the queen of clubs to come down doubleton or for the hearts to break 4-4.

Playing on spades may allow the defenders to cash out if hearts are 5-3 but it leaves us many more options when they are 4-4. We therefore lead the king of spades at Trick 2. West takes his ace immediately as East follows with the eight.

After considerable thought, West switches to the ten of clubs. East plays the two and we win with the jack. When we then play a club to the king West follows with the queen.

We lead the queen of diamonds and East follows low. It's decision time. **Should we take the diamond finesse or go up with the ace and play for the clubs to break 3-3?**

I usually play very quickly but this decision takes me an eternity. I eventually play the ace of diamonds. When both defenders follow to the ace of clubs I am caught smiling by the Vugraph camera.

This is the full hand:

```
                    ♠ Q J 5 3
                    ♡ 9 6 3 2
                    ◇ Q 6 5
                    ♣ K 9
   ♠ A 9 2        ┌─────────┐      ♠ 10 8 7 4
   ♡ A 8 7 5      │    N    │      ♡ Q J 10 4
   ◇ K 4 3        │ W     E │      ◇ 7 2
   ♣ Q 10 8       │    S    │      ♣ 5 4 2
                  └─────────┘
                    ♠ K 6
                    ♡ K
                    ◇ A J 10 9 8
                    ♣ A J 7 6 3
```

Eddie Kantar once wrote a learned article explaining why it is best to play the jack at Trick 1 in the position East faced. Although partner is deceived about the position of the ten he will always know it is safe to continue the suit (as declarer will have K-Q-10 or K-10), which is the message third hand wants to send. On the actual hand, West fatally looked elsewhere as he could not read the heart position.

At the other table, the British North-South play in a diamond partscore so we gain 10 IMPs.

Tony and Andrew get slightly the better of the second half at our table. We win the match but it's another close one — 17-13 in VPs. We have won all three matches on this first day but we are only 5 VPs above average and there are two teams, Sweden and Italy, ahead of us. It is all very close as one would expect at this early stage. Over dinner tonight it is decided that Eric and I will play only one match tomorrow, the middle one against the Swedes. That means a lie-in and a swim in the morning and perhaps some sightseeing before dinner.

Bob Hamman

DAY TWO

Match 4 vs. Canada

When we are sitting out I try to stay well clear of the tournament. The objective is to relax completely and I cannot do that if I am around the playing rooms or the Vugraph Theatre.

Just a few minutes before our first pair finish playing, I arrive in the concourse where everyone mills about before and after matches. They comment that the Canucks have played well and the match seems fairly flat. And so it turns out — another 16-14 win, but we drop to fourth place as Poland scores a big victory to overtake us.

The Canadians: Mittelman, Kokish, Silver, Molson, Baran, Gitelman

I always enjoy playing against the Swedes. They are all good guys and tough opponents. They also make you think as they are extremely innovative in terms of the development of systems. Eric and I have picked up more than one neat idea from them over the years. One thing I do find interesting is that Swedish partnerships seldom seem to last long, although I have no idea why that should be.

Our opponents today are Gunnar Hallberg and Bjorn Axelson. To emphasize my point, since we played this match Gunnar has not only found himself a new partner but a new country — he will be representing England when we next meet.

This is a set of boards with plenty of potential for swings. Midway through the match, with both sides vulnerable, we pick up:

♠ A 6 3   ♡ A J 6   ◇ A J 7 5 4 2   ♣ A

Axelson, on our right, opens proceedings with **three spades** and we are faced with a fairly common dilemma — Three Notrump or Four Diamonds, with Pass and Double as outside contenders. **What would you do?**

Bidding over preempts is never easy and always involves an element of guesswork. Readers may be disappointed to hear that I have no magic solution to offer except to say that 3NT is often the safest choice. For one thing, there is no trump stack to run into.

None of the options here is particularly appealing and **three notrump** looks as likely to be right as any of the alternatives.

Partner advances with **four hearts**, which we have agreed to play as natural and constructive.

How would you proceed from here?

Eric and I are known for having discussed thousands of bidding sequences but, perhaps surprisingly, this is not one of them. Are you confident that you and your regular partner would agree on the meaning of Four Notrump? I elect to bid Four Notrump, intending it as Roman Key-Card Blackwood agreeing hearts. Unfortunately, Eric thinks that Four Notrump is natural and passes.

There is logic in using 4NT as a natural bid here. For example, you do not want to be forced to five-of-a-minor if your 3NT is based on running tricks in a minor and a couple of outside stoppers. There may well be ten tricks in both notrump and the suit contract.

If Four Notrump is natural, you need another way to agree hearts and ask for key cards. It is very difficult to bid slams accurately without some kind of ace/control asking device, so we always try to have RKCB available. At the conclusion of this match, we agree to play 4NT as natural and the lowest change of suit as RKCB agreeing advancer's suit. One reason for including this hand here is to illustrate that everyone has system misunderstandings, even those playing at the highest level.

Fortunately, playing in Four Notrump is not a complete disaster on this occasion. Eric's hand is:

♠ 5
♡ K 10 9 4 3
◊ 6 3
♣ K Q 5 4 3

♠ A 6 3
♡ A J 6
◊ A J 7 5 4 2
♣ A

It seems logical to play the partner of the preemptor for the queen of hearts. When that is the right decision we score up our contract for a flat board.

Six Hearts is unbeatable but not exactly laydown. At none of the sixteen tables in play does anyone get there, though. Two pairs reach Six Diamonds and one is allowed to make it on a bizarre misdefense. Most of the rest reach a notrump game and make nine or ten tricks.

Gunnar Hallberg

This is not a well-played match and either team may yet live to regret some of the opportunities it missed. We retain our 100% winning record — 17-13 again. I bid our teammates good fortune in the final match of the day and set out with Shirlee for our first up-close look at Beijing. . .

Match 6 vs. Norway

While our teammates play the final match of the day, Shirlee, Eric and I take a taxi into the center of Beijing. It's not a long journey, perhaps only five miles or so to the south of our peaceful retreat. But the serenity disappears the moment we emerge from the park.

The view from the taxi soon gets monotonous — row after row after row of identical apartment buildings. The journey is slow going despite an eight-lane highway. Beijing is home to some twelve million people and it would be easy to believe that every one of them was heading southwards this afternoon. As we travel deeper and deeper into the heart of the city we are enveloped, on all sides and high above, by swathes of concrete and glass. Then, suddenly, we arrive. The taxi deposits us on the edge of a concrete desert — Tiananmen Square — surrounded on all sides by gargantuan modern buildings.

Eric in Beijing

We elect to delay investigation of the Forbidden City until we have more time. Today was only intended as a reconnaissance trip. I love to visit new places and today has proved a real eye-opener. Beijing is nothing like I had imagined it would be and I look forward to further investigation as time permits. A couple of the Swedish players who have been here before told us to try some of the little restaurants in the cobweb of alleys running between the main highways and to check out the little antique markets. I certainly hope to do so but my senses have taken all the battering they can stand for one day.

We return to the hotel in time to join the rest of our team for the scoring. The Norwegians are a very young team with tremendous talent. They are capable of beating anyone on their day but, as our teammates report over dinner, this day was not theirs.

However, our side was not immune from silly mistakes either and the boys are a trifle disappointed with their 20-10 victory. Still, it is our biggest win so far and we remain unbeaten. Only the Canadians are ahead of us now. Not that we are in any sort of commanding position — we have 103 VPs with 90 average. The team in sixth place have 89 so one big loss would drop us right back to where we started.

I don't linger for drinks after dinner this evening as we are scheduled to play in all three matches tomorrow.

Jeff in Beijing

DAY THREE

3

Match 7 vs Italy

We have played the Italians many times over the years and know most of their top pairs well. Alfredo Versace and Lorenzo Lauria are good friends and they are at the other table in this match. They both have a great sense of humor and we have shared lots of laughs with them over the years, both at and away from the table. At Bermuda 2000, Norberto Bocchi and Giorgio Duboin were tremendous against us and I'm glad they're missing this year. The Italian pair at our table today are Arturo Franco and Dano De Falco, both Bermuda Bowl winners during the great Blue Team era.

The match goes fairly well and, with both vulnerable on the final deal of the match, our hand is:

$\spadesuit$ A J 9 8 2 $\heartsuit$ A 8 5 $\diamondsuit$ K 10 $\clubsuit$ A J 4

We deal and open with a strong **one club**. Partner makes a natural positive with **one heart** and we continue with **one spade**. Eric raises to **two spades** and we show our fit for his suit with **three hearts**. When he continues with Three Spades it's time to assess what we know. It sounds as if we have two 5-3 fits so it's just a question of which major to choose. Our minor-suit

---

holdings suggest that we want be declarer rather than dummy. We have no extras, having already opened with a Strong Club, so a simple raise to game seems right — **four spades.** Thus ends a fairly straightforward auction.

WEST	NORTH	EAST	SOUTH
De Falco	Eric	Franco	Us
			1♣[1]
pass	1♡	pass	1♠
pass	2♠	pass	3♡
pass	3♠	pass	4♠
all pass			

1. Artificial, 16+.

West leads the six of clubs and dummy hits with:

♠ K Q 5
♡ J 6 4 3 2
◊ Q 8 5 2
♣ 8

```
        N
  W         E
        S
```

♣ 6 led

♠ A J 9 8 2
♡ A 8 5
◊ K 10
♣ A J 4

Given favorable breaks we can make ten tricks via five trumps, two aces, one diamond and two club ruffs.

We capture East's king of clubs lead with the ace and immediately ruff a club. A diamond to the king wins and it is tempting to take a second club ruff now. **Can you see a better alternative?**

If trumps break it probably won't matter how we time the play. What if West has four spades to the ten, though? Maybe then we will need to score the small spades in hand by ruffing diamonds. To pave the way for this we should lead our second diamond now.

West covers the ten of diamonds with the jack. It looks right to duck this. We know who has the ace of diamonds and that knowledge may come in useful later, when we try to ruff two diamonds.

On winning with the jack of diamonds, West exits with a trump.

If East has ♠10xxx then we can score five trumps in hand by ruffing a diamond and then exiting in hearts. We will then make two trump winners with the jack-nine tenace later. If it is West who holds the trump length, though, the defenders may be able to engineer a trump promotion. **How might we avoid this?**

If West has a doubleton king or queen of hearts, he will have to unblock his honor under the ace in order to get his partner on lead in the endgame. If we delay playing hearts, the need to do this will become obvious. Playing off the ace of hearts right now may catch West napping.

When we play a heart to the ace, West follows with the seven. We can now ruff a club with dummy's last trump and return to hand with a diamond ruff. The ace does not appear, so we know that it is East who holds the defenders' last diamond. As we feared, East discards a club when we cash the ace of spades. The position is now something like this:

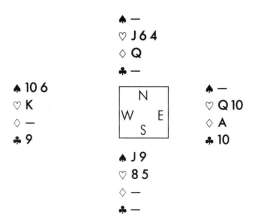

We exit with a heart which West has to win. Whether he returns a trump or a club, the nine of spades will be our tenth trick.

Observe the difference if West had unblocked the king of hearts. East would then be able to win Trick 10. He would cash his second heart winner or his ace of diamonds, West throwing his club. A plain-suit lead through our jack-nine of trumps at Trick 12 would then promote the ten of spades into the setting trick. The full deal is:

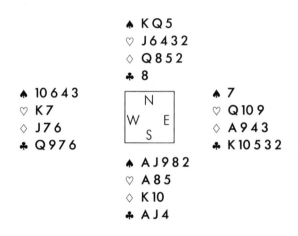

```
              ♠ KQ5
              ♡ J6432
              ◇ Q852
              ♣ 8
  ♠ 10643              ♠ 7
  ♡ K7         N       ♡ Q109
  ◇ J76     W     E    ◇ A943
  ♣ Q976       S       ♣ K10532
              ♠ AJ982
              ♡ A85
              ◇ K10
              ♣ AJ4
```

At the other table, the play started similarly except that declarer covered the jack of diamonds with the queen at Trick 4. East also returned a trump and declarer crossed to the ace of hearts but our West unblocked the king. The subsequent trump promotion meant one down and a 12-IMP swing.

Dano De Falco

We win the match 61-41 which translates to 19-11 in VPs.

With the first Round Robin complete we are fairly well placed. The group table looks something like this:

1	Canada	124
2	USA	122
3	Sweden	117
4	Poland	111
5	Italy	109
6	Great Britain	105
7	Norway	83
8	New Zealand	69

Match 8 vs. Poland

This is a tough struggle with some good bridge played by both sides. The deals, however, are relatively uninteresting and the scores low. The 22-22 IMP tie is an acceptable result for both teams. However, Italy thrashes New Zealand 24-6, closing the gap significantly.

Marek Szymanowski

Match 9 vs. New Zealand

Now it's our turn. This match offers us the opportunity to consolidate our position. As expected, the Kiwis are struggling and playing now only for pride. Our opponents, Lionel Wright and Malcolm Mayer, use a really complex relay system. Pairs are required to pre-submit their systems and theirs is over 100 pages long!

For some reason, we struggle in this match. As it draws to a close, with neither side vulnerable, we are dealt:

♠ K973   ♡ 6   ◇ AK1083   ♣ AQ2

Mayer, on our right, opens a 15-17 **one notrump**.

We have been toying with a new defense to a strong notrump (imaginatively named Meckwell) but we are not using it yet. Our choices today are Two Diamonds, showing spades and another suit, or a penalty double.

This hand has a high defense-to-offense ratio and a good opening lead, so the **double** looks to be the better option.

LHO passes, which is alerted as forcing opener to redouble and may include a wide range of hands. Our partnership style in these auctions when the opponents pass or redouble conventionally is that Eric's pass shows values and creates a force. He is expected to run immediately with a bad hand (2◇/2♡/2♠ show at least a five-card suit and he bids 2♣ with either clubs or no long suit, scramble style).

When it gets back to him, opener obediently **redoubles**. We pass, so does leftie, and partner removes himself to **two hearts**. **What do you think of this development?**

None of our options look particularly attractive, but leaving partner to play in what is surely only a 5-1 heart fit does not feel right. Of the other options, 2NT is clearly wrong since it is bound to be doubled and partner has already said that he doesn't think we can make seven tricks, let alone eight. Three Diamonds may well be right, but it puts all of our eggs in one basket. The third possibility and probably the best is **two spades**. If this gets doubled quickly, we can always re-evaluate and bid Three Diamonds on the next round.

Both LHO and partner pass and, somewhat surprisingly, opener jumps to **three notrump**. **Have you had enough or do you fancy a crack at this?**

Whilst it is true that we've bid our hand already, don't you have that gut feeling that the opponents have misjudged? Plus, we have a surprise lead coming. Assuming they don't redouble, it's only a 4-IMP loss if they make it, with a much higher yield if they go down two or three tricks. At IMPs, doubling game contracts can be safer and more profitable than doubling partscores. Watch out for the blue card though.

This has been the eventful auction:

WEST	NORTH	EAST	SOUTH
Us	*Wright*	*Eric*	*Mayer*
			1NT
dbl	pass[1]	pass	redbl
pass	pass	2♡	pass
2♠	pass	pass	3NT
dbl	all pass		

1. Forces a redouble.

What should we lead?

♠ K 9 7 3 ♡ 6 ◇ A K 10 8 3 ♣ A Q 2

It's only a question of which diamond. Starting with a top one seems best in case one of them has some useful doubleton such as Q-J, Q-9 or J-9.

We choose the king of diamonds and this is what we see:

```
                      ♠ Q 6 5
                      ♡ Q 7 5 2
                      ◇ J 7 5
                      ♣ J 5 3
        ♠ K 9 7 3     ┌─────────┐
        ♡ 6           │    N    │
        ◇ A K 10 8 3  │ W     E │
        ♣ A Q 2       │    S    │
                      └─────────┘
```

Eric follows with the two of diamonds, standard count. So, partner has three diamonds. It doesn't seem to matter whether we play a low diamond or the ace at Trick 2. **Or does it?**

There is one other possibility — that partner was dealt the doubleton Q-2 of diamonds. Clearly, if that should be the case, cashing the ace next would be costly. We therefore play the three of diamonds next, giving a suit preference signal for clubs.

Meckwell

Sure enough, partner wins with the queen of diamonds and returns the nine of clubs. We win with the queen and cash our diamond winners. Declarer cannot afford to bare his ace of spades, but keeping two does not work either. We cash the ace of clubs and play a third round, removing dummy's entry in that suit while the hearts are still blocked. We must still come to the king of spades at the end. Wow! Four down. For a somewhat speculative double, that turned out rather well. This is the full deal:

```
                    ♠ Q 6 5
                    ♡ Q 7 5 2
                    ◇ J 7 5
                    ♣ J 5 3
    ♠ K 9 7 3                        ♠ 10 8 2
    ♡ 6              ┌─────────┐     ♡ 10 9 8 4 3
    ◇ A K 10 8 3     │    N    │     ◇ Q 2
    ♣ A Q 2         W│         │E    ♣ 9 6 4
                     │    S    │
                    └─────────┘
                    ♠ A J 4
                    ♡ A K J
                    ◇ 9 8 4
                    ♣ K 10 8 7
```

South's decision to bid 3NT was misguided. Not that doubling Two Spades would have fared much better — we are cold for nine tricks in that contract. South's best option was to pass, but they were probably in a forcing auction. Had he chosen 2NT he would have escaped for minus 150, though, as we could not have doubled that.

Alas, this board is our only good result in the match. We have suffered our first defeat, and in a match we were looking to win heavily. New Zealand wins by 10 IMPs, 17-13 in VPs.

More bad news is that Great Britain hammered Norway 25-5 and at the end of the third day the scores are: Canada 155, USA 150, Italy 147, Sweden 146, Britain 145 and Poland 142 with the other two teams out of the race.

Bobby Levin

DAY FOUR

Match 10 vs. Great Britain

The Brit's big win in the last match yesterday has catapulted them right back into contention so this has become a crucial match. We once again find ourselves pitted against Forrester-Robson on Vugraph.

On the very first deal of the day, with neither side vulnerable, we pick up this rather unappealing collection:

♠ 10 7   ♡ 8 7 5   ◇ A Q 8 7   ♣ J 8 7 3

We pass as dealer and hear **pass-one spade-pass** back to us.

Playing Precision, partner's One Spade is limited to a maximum of 15 HCP so there is no chance of game for our side. We could therefore pass and leave partner to play his 5-2 fit at the one-level but that would be poor tactics.

It is always right to make life as tough for the opponents as possible. Passing lets them into the auction too easily — who knows, if partner is light they may even have a game. As we are non-vulnerable responding is easy — it's only 50 a trick if we go minus. A **one notrump** response is quite likely to keep them out of the bidding. We duly buy the contract in 1NT and West (Forrester) attacks with the six of spades. Eric puts down:

♠ K Q 8 5
♡ A 10
◇ 10 6 3
♣ K 10 6 2

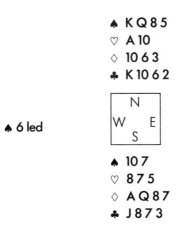

♠ 6 led

N
W E
S

♠ 10 7
♡ 8 7 5
◇ A Q 8 7
♣ J 8 7 3

I see. Partner's One Spade was a good tactical move, third seat non-vulnerable. The opponents have the balance of points, just, and an eight-card heart fit, so they rate to be able to make a partscore. Going down in this contract may prove to be okay but let's forget about that for now. Planning the play in low-level contracts like this is never easy. It is frequently difficult or even impossible to foresee the ending as there are too many unknown variables. The best strategy is a one-step-at-a-time approach, with constant re-evaluation as the play progresses and we learn more about the layout.

Andrew Robson

We have a decision right away. As dummy advertised five spades in the bidding, West is likely to have a reasonable holding in the suit to have led it. Playing a spade honor at Trick 1 will put us in serious trouble if East holds something like A-x. In addition, running the opening lead to the ten virtually kills the suit for the defense if West has led from an ace-jack holding.

We therefore play low from dummy. Robson wins with the jack of spades and shifts to the jack of diamonds.

That's not such an unfriendly development. We can be fairly sure that hearts are 4-4 — both defenders have been in and both have chosen to attack a different suit.

We cover the jack of diamonds and our queen wins. We could attack clubs straight away, but it seems better to start with the ten of spades. If the defenders grab their ace immediately then we'll be able to cash two spade tricks later. More likely, they'll allow the ten of spades to win and we can then switch to clubs with a spade trick already in the bag.

We lead the ten of spades and, as expected, it holds.

We now have four tricks. **How should we play the clubs?**

Stealing one club trick may enable us to scramble seven tricks via three diamonds, two spades, a club and a heart. Let's think about the distribution. It looks as if West started with 4-4 in the majors which leaves seven major-suit cards in the East hand. Robson also appears to have long diamonds. If he has five then that leaves room for only one club.

It seems that West has the ace of spades and something in hearts. As he failed to open the bidding he cannot, therefore, also have both club honors.

Our best shot seems to be a club to the king. Lo and behold, this drops East's queen. We play a club to the jack and West's ace, win the heart switch, cross to the ace of diamonds, and take the proven finesse against West's nine of clubs for seven tricks.

At the other table, our teammates stop in Two Hearts and score eight tricks — 5 IMPs to the good guys.

The match progresses slowly (as is always the case when Andrew is at the table) with neither side gaining much of an advantage. Early in the second half, with neither side vulnerable, we pick up:

♠ Q432　♡ KQ82　◇ AJ3　♣ A8

Eric opens **one spade** — 10-15 HCP and a five-card suit. It is obvious to start with our forcing raise — Jacoby **two notrump**. Partner's **three diamonds** rebid shows a shortage in that suit. **How good do you think our hand is?**

Our partnership philosophy on slam bidding is to play our game hands in game — four of a major, not five and 3NT, not four. In general, if we are going to be wrong we want to miss on the low side. There are lots of ways to win IMPs with plus 680. So we don't bid a lot of slams in auctions where it's just a guess if partner has the right hand.

This hand is far too good for a conservative approach, though. Partner's diamond shortage increases the value of both our club doubleton and our heart honors since he will almost certainly have at least three cards in each of those suits.

We could go slowly with a Three Hearts cuebid but we are good enough to take control and simplify the auction. We roll out Roman Key Card Blackwood — **four notrump** — and hear a **five hearts** response, showing two of the five key cards. We are off a key card — **would you bid the slam or sign off in Five Spades?**

I choose the aggressive action — **six spades**.

This is certainly the right option this time, as partner's hand is:

♠ A K J 9 8   ♡ J 10 6   ♢ 6   ♣ K J 6 4

Slam is excellent despite a combined holding of only 29 HCP and no long suits. The hands fit well and only exceptionally bad breaks would jeopardize the contract. Eric has no trouble collecting twelve tricks, which brings in 11 IMPs when the Brits at the other table stop at the five-level.

The match seems to be closing out with a series of dull game hands when, with neither side vulnerable, we are greeted with this picture gallery:

♠ A 7 2   ♡ A K Q J 5 3   ♢ A 7   ♣ A 7

We open with an artificial strong One Club and hear a natural and preemptive jump to Three Spades on our left. Partner's Double shows any hand with 8+ HCP. RHO passes and it's our turn. **How do you feel about this hand?**

Because of the high level of the preempt we don't have many options: Four Hearts would be non-forcing and Four Notrump would show both minors. We basically have to bid what we think we can make. There is one small clue that partner's hand will be suitable — with spade values he might have bid 3NT, rather than doubling.

Just taking a stab at the grand slam is very tempting — it rates to have good play opposite most hands and to be laydown enough of the time to make it worth bidding. We therefore jump to Seven Hearts and await the sight of dummy.

As it happens, it all hinges on Forrester's choice of opening lead. His actual selection, a trump, is not the winning one from his perspective. Dummy has:

♠ 8 6
♡ 8 7 2
♢ K J 9 5 4 2
♣ K

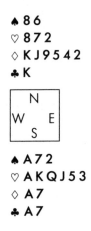

♠ A 7 2
♡ A K Q J 5 3
♢ A 7
♣ A 7

Although trumps break 3-1, diamonds split evenly and we are quickly claiming our grand slam. At the other table, the British North jumps to only Six Hearts after a similar start to the auction. 11 IMPs added to our tally.

An opening club lead would have removed dummy's outside entry and we would have been forced into the diamond finesse. As East held ♢Qxx, we would have finished three down. That would have resulted in 14 IMPs the other way.

Edgar Kaplan and Dick Freeman

That 25 IMPs is worth five Victory Points. We win the match by 67-50 — 18-12 VPs and go to the top of the leader board when Poland beats Canada by the same margin. Neither of the other contenders fare well — Sweden draws with their arch-rivals, Norway, while Italy loses to the New Zealanders.

Match 11 vs. Canada

Eric and I sit this one out. The plan is for us to relax now and come back fully charged for the final three matches, one tonight and two tomorrow. Shirlee and I were originally planning another trip into the city, but with things so close I prefer to relax in my room watching golf on television while she is happy to take advantage of the hotel pool.

I enjoy a fascinating two hours of live golf from some European tournament and it is a struggle to tear myself away when it is time to go downstairs to meet our teammates for the scoring. I am a great believer in the importance of team spirit and togetherness, though, so I always try to be present at the end of matches. By all accounts, both teams have played some superb bridge but we manage a narrow victory (17-13) while New Zealand also wins yet again, denting Polish hopes. Although our position can hardly be described as comfortable, we can see a little daylight behind us. The leading scores are USA 185, Canada 180, Sweden 178, Italy 173, Poland 172, Britain 172.

Buoyed by their performance this afternoon, our other pairs feel they are in the groove and are keen to keep going. We have no objection and Eric and I head for an early dinner in the hotel restaurant while they do battle.

Having eaten well, we are in good spirits. We are chatting over a quiet beer in the hotel bar when news begins to filter through to us from American supporters leaving the Vugraph Theatre that things are not going well. In fact, they are going disastrously badly. The final debacle is by 87-39 which represents a 5-25 loss.

Bobby Wolff

As the rest of the results filter in it is clear that we will have our work well and truly cut out tomorrow. With Poland and Great Britain both winning by considerable margins, we have dropped out of the top four with just two matches remaining — against Norway and the old enemy, Italy. The overnight scores are Sweden 203, Canada 201, Poland 197, Britain 192, USA 190, Italy 182 with Norway and New Zealand well out of it.

DAY FIVE

5

Match 13 vs. Norway

We didn't play against the Norwegians the first time around but I recall that they did not perform well. Indeed, they have not played up to their potential throughout the event. This would not be a good moment for them suddenly to find their form.

The opponents at our table are the top Norwegian pair, Tor Helness and Geir Helgemo. Both are great guys and good friends. I love to play blackjack with them and we've had especially good luck in London casinos together. The last time we were there, I recall that we were asked to reduce the frequency and volume of our high-fives and excessive celebrations.

It doesn't look like we'll be playing blackjack together in Beijing, though, as they are obviously going home early. Right now, we're in serious danger of catching the same flight.

The boards are difficult and the advantage at our table swings both ways although we seem to be gaining the upper hand. Towards the end of the match, with both sides vulnerable, our hand is:

♠ 10 4   ♡ Q 3   ◇ 5   ♣ A J 10 9 7 6 5 4

Partner opens **one heart** and RHO passes. Many pairs playing Standard would have to start with a forcing notrump but we have an alternative option. We play jump shifts as invitational but non-forcing. We are not quite worth a jump to **three clubs** but the eighth club is a persuasive feature and it's easy to talk ourselves into the overbid. Partner rebids **three notrump**. **Do you pass?**

Although not unexpected, this is not the ideal development. For 3NT to be the best contract Eric will need just the right hand. We are having a fairly good set and the idea of losing three or four hundred in a hopeless game does not appeal.

> I chicken out, retreat to **four clubs**, and push the bidding tray back under the screen. I comment to Tor, who is my screen-mate and sitting West, that "somebody on the other side of the screen is sighing heavily."

I guess bidding was not the right option.

When the tray comes back, Eric has raised to game. This has been the auction:

WEST	NORTH	EAST	SOUTH
Helness	*Eric*	*Helgemo*	*Us*
	1♡	pass	3♣
pass	3NT	pass	4♣
pass	5♣	all pass	

Tor leads the seven of diamonds and dummy appears with:

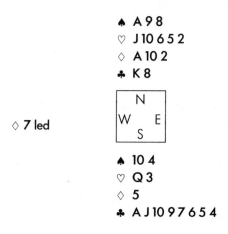

♠ A 9 8
♡ J 10 6 5 2
♢ A 10 2
♣ K 8

◇ 7 led

♠ 10 4
♡ Q 3
♢ 5
♣ A J 10 9 7 6 5 4

It is immediately clear that we are in the wrong game — 3NT is likely to be an easy make. This is the type of hand on which you cannot think for an age at Trick 1. Good defenders are very quick to realize when you have a problem.

> When I saw dummy, my immediate thought was, 'Well, they're going to figure it out. Maybe they won't if I stick in the ten of diamonds.'

East wins Trick 1 with the queen of diamonds and, not realizing the urgency of his position, returns a diamond. Our prospects are suddenly much rosier. We throw a heart from hand and win the trick with dummy's ace of diamonds. When we then play a heart at Trick 3 the defenders have no answer. This is the full deal:

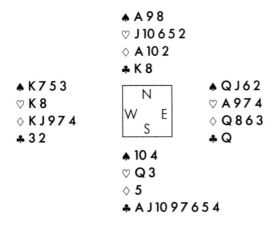

                    ♠ A 9 8
                    ♡ J 10 6 5 2
                    ◇ A 10 2
                    ♣ K 8
    ♠ K 7 5 3   ♠ Q J 6 2
    ♡ K 8   ┌──────────┐   ♡ A 9 7 4
    ◇ K J 9 7 4   │   N   │   ◇ Q 8 6 3
    ♣ 3 2   │ W   E │   ♣ Q
                   │   S   │
                   └──────────┘
                    ♠ 10 4
                    ♡ Q 3
                    ◇ 5
                    ♣ A J 10 9 7 6 5 4

If East wins with the first heart with the ace, we will be able to ruff out the king and later pitch our spade loser on the jack of hearts.

In fact, East ducks the first heart to his partner's king. West switches to a spade but we win with the ace and lead the jack of hearts. East covers and we ruff away his ace. The ace of clubs and a club to the king draw the trumps, and our spade loser is discarded on the ten of hearts. Contract made — plus 600.

We still lose an IMP on the deal, as the Norwegian pair at the other table play 3NT and score an easy 630.

This was a cute hand and is one of my all-time favorites. The winning play is really very simple if you think of it, and think of it quickly.

(Jeff's declarer play on this hand won him the IBPA's *Le Bridgeur* Award for the 'Best Played Hand' of 1997.)

The Norwegians played much better this time around. We win the match, but only by 54-50 and thus 16-14 in VPs. The good news is that Poland and Canada both lose. The bad news is that their defeats are against the Brits and Italy, so we actually lose ground slightly on fourth place and we now have the Italians, our remaining opponents, breathing down our necks.

With one match remaining, the leading scores are Sweden 220, Canada 210, Britain 210, Poland 209, USA 206, Italy 203. While we take on Italy, Canada plays the Brits and Sweden squares off against Poland. Still just about any four of these six could survive.

Match 14 vs. Italy

Once again, Versace-Lauria are at the other table. Our opponents are another pair of rising young stars, Andrea Buratti and Massimo Lanzarotti. This is the same foursome who won Italy's first World Championship in twenty-two years at the 1998 Rosenblum in Lille.

If we can win this match, we must be in with a decent chance since Canada and Britain, both only 4 VPs ahead of us, are playing each other. In normal circumstances, even a small loss might suffice, but we are only 3 VPs ahead of the Italians and we surely cannot afford to let them overtake us. That would be asking too much.

The first deal is a flat 3NT and then, with only our side vulnerable, we pick up this promising collection:

♠ J 5 ♡ A K 8 6 2 ◇ A Q 9 8 ♣ A 9

RHO (Lanzarotti) deals and opens **one notrump**, 12-14. We play penalty doubles of a weak notrump and that seems to be the clear choice on this hand. Buratti, on my left, redoubles and that is passed back to me. **Do you have any thoughts?**

We double a weak notrump fairly light (14+ HCP) so we tend not to pass partner's double without some values. It seems logical that the same principles should also apply when the responder redoubles, so it sounds like the opponents have had a misunderstanding about the meaning of the redouble. If so, then Christmas has surely come early.

Any thoughts about what we should lead?

Should we do anything unusual just because this is a redoubled contract? The fourth best of our longest and strongest looks like the safest lead...

This turns out to be the full hand:

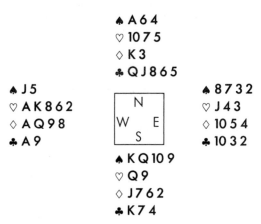

```
              ♠ A 6 4
              ♡ 10 7 5
              ◇ K 3
              ♣ Q J 8 6 5
  ♠ J 5                        ♠ 8 7 3 2
  ♡ A K 8 6 2   ┌─────────┐   ♡ J 4 3
  ◇ A Q 9 8     │ N       │   ◇ 10 5 4
  ♣ A 9         │ W     E │   ♣ 10 3 2
                │   S     │
                └─────────┘
              ♠ K Q 10 9
              ♡ Q 9
              ◇ J 7 6 2
              ♣ K 7 4
```

Declarer wins the low heart lead with the queen and plays on clubs. All we can do is cash four hearts, a diamond and our club ace to hold the contract to seven tricks. East/West minus 560 represents a 10-IMP loss when teammates score plus 110 in Two Spades at the other table.

If you chose to lead a top heart, partner's count signal showing three would be a welcome sight. After three rounds of hearts partner would switch to a diamond. Whether you duck this to the king or win, cash your hearts and then play a second diamond yourself, you will be able to score a second diamond winner when you get in with the ace of clubs. Declarer then makes just five tricks and your plus 600 is worth 12 IMPs. Great — a 22-IMP swing on an opening lead to start off the match.

How one copes mentally with disasters is critical to success. It's similar to a golfer who has just made a double bogey. Dwelling on that previous hole just produces a bad tee shot on the next one. Maintaining concentration on the job at hand is vital. I try to use disasters as motivation to work harder. You must stay positive and focused but, of course, that is much easier said than done.

Momentum is a big factor, particularly in reasonably long matches. When things are going wrong I tend to be more cautious. When they are going well, I am more aggressive. Doing something outrageous in an attempt to recover the loss on the next deal seldom works. The usual result is that your position gets even worse.   Be patient and wait for an opportunity to come. Things will turn naturally. You have to accept that bridge is not a perfect game — it's a game of mistakes. It's rare that I play a session without making at least one mistake, or having a misunderstanding with partner, etc. Your opponents will make them too. You just have to be alert and ready to capitalize when they do.

As the match wears on, nothing particularly good seems to be happening.   With four boards remaining and neither side vulnerable, we deal and pick up:

♠ J 10 9 6 5 3   ♡ K 4   ◇ K 7 3   ♣ 5 4

If we want to open this hand with a Weak Two bid then we must do so via a Multi Two Diamonds in our system. The other vaguely sensible options are Three Spades and Pass. How do you feel about each of these choices?

Our partnership philosophy is that, if possible, one should always make some call other than 'Pass'. It's something about which we feel strongly and it has stood us in good stead over the years.

The winning Italian team at the 2000 Olympiad

With a hand like this, passing will lead to many later bidding problems. Sometimes you'll even have to guess whether to bid at the four-level! Clearly, that is much more dangerous than opening with a weak two. If you open, you presumably won't have any future problems. The remaining decisions will all be partner's and he will have a reasonable idea of your hand. As far as opening Three Spades goes... Zia is the big advocate of the style whereby three-level openings are weaker than weak twos but that's not for us. Our feeling is that preempts at the three-level should contain reasonable playing strength. This hand certainly does not qualify.

The variation of the Multi Two Diamonds opening that Eric and I use has no strong options. It always shows a weak two opening in one of the majors.

Having opened **two diamonds**, we hear the auction continue **pass-pass-double**. Partner is very likely to have long diamonds and we seem to have good support for that suit. In most cases, once you have preempted you will not bid again freely, but increasing the preemptive barrage whenever possible is a good tactic. A raise to **three diamonds** therefore seems right now.

LHO **doubles** this and, rather surprisingly, RHO removes to Three Spades. That's an interesting development and you would not need to be clairvoyant to guess leftie's next bid now. Right — **three notrump**. The full hand is:

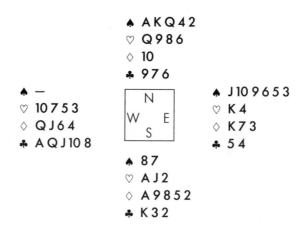

           ♠ A K Q 4 2
           ♡ Q 9 8 6
           ◊ 10
           ♣ 9 7 6

♠ —   ♠ J 10 9 6 5 3
♡ 10 7 5 3   ♡ K 4
◊ Q J 6 4   ◊ K 7 3
♣ A Q J 10 8   ♣ 5 4

           ♠ 8 7
           ♡ A J 2
           ◊ A 9 8 5 2
           ♣ K 3 2

The bidding raises a number of points that regular partnerships might wish to address. Eric's pass of Two Diamonds looks right — he can be fairly confident that our suit is spades and playing doubled in a 6-0 fit with very few high-cards is not likely to produce a good result. Perhaps our assumption of long diamonds opposite is therefore flawed. The raise to Three Diamonds certainly offered the opponents a shot at a large penalty — a trump lead would defeat the contract by three tricks for -500.

North also misjudged — he thought that the double of Three Diamonds was responsive.

Three Notrump is not a thing of beauty but the favorable heart position renders it unbeatable. On the actual queen of clubs lead, declarer had no trouble taking nine tricks via three spades, four hearts and a trick in each minor.

At the other table, East also elected to open with a Weak Two. South did not feel his hand was quite worth a takeout double of the natural Two Spades opening and what could North do?

He passed it out and the defense was not optimal, so declarer escaped with seven tricks — another 8 IMPs in the 'Out' column.

When you play against world-class players you will lose IMPs on some deals because they bid or play well. You must accept such losses without worrying about them. To win at this level, you need to avoid losing IMPs on boards such as this one, where the opponents do nothing good.

The scoring is as depressing as the match. We lose but only just, 28-32, which is 14-16 in VPs. That keeps us one Victory Point ahead of the Italians at least. Will it be enough to overhaul any of the teams ahead of us, though?

Mario Lanzarotti

We'll know soon enough. The Poles and Swedes finish just after us and we join them for the scoring. The Poles are jubilant — they win 21-9 to qualify comfortably.

We all wander into the Vugraph Theater to watch the conclusion of the Canada-Great Britain match as the last deal is placed on the table in the Open Room. The Canucks are winning comfortably, but the commentators have worked out that the Brits need to gain 1 IMP on the last deal to overhaul us and claim the final spot in the knockout stage. The Canadians have an indifferent result in the Closed Room, where play has already finished, and things look bleak. The bidding progresses normally and it looks certain that the British team will get their IMP. Forrester and Robson join us to watch the final action. They're friends and we congratulate them and wish them good luck for the rest of the event.

> I am sure I am not alone in thinking of the long flight home. On the screen, something goes wrong with the British pair's defense. They've dropped a trick but even that is not enough for us. Then one of them panics and crashes his partner's trump trick. The Canadian declarer has made his doubled contract and the American fans all around us are screaming and shouting. Looking back on it, I'm sure I was too. There is pandemonium in the Vugraph Theater as the victorious Canadians enter to massive cheers. The 10 IMPs they gain on

Andrea Buratti

the deal means that they win 21-9, which enables them to leapfrog both Sweden and Poland to win the group, thus giving them the choice of opponents in the quarterfinal.

Remarkably, we're still alive...

The final group table looks like this:

1	Canada	231
2	Poland	230
3	Sweden	229
4	USA	220
5	Great Britain	219
6	Italy	219
7	Norway	171
8	New Zealand	161

Half of the field will be on their way home soon but there is no morning session scheduled for tomorrow so everyone attends the players' party. At well past midnight, grateful American players are heard thanking their northern neighbors with an impromptu rendition of *O, Canada*.

In the other group, the other American team fails to progress. The winner of that group, France, chooses to play Sweden while Canada selects surprise qualifier South Africa as its quarterfinal opponent. That leaves Poland to play the host country, China, while we will be pitted against Brazil.

2

The Quarter-Final

We have played against the Brazilians many times over the years. They beat us in the 1991 quarter-final in Yokohama, when they were the defending champions, and they reached the final of the 50th Anniversary Bermuda Bowl in 2000, so we do not have any illusions that this will be an easy match.

The Brazilian anchor pair, Gabriel Chagas and Marcelo Branco, are truly world class. Both have won the Triple Crown (the Bermuda Bowl, the Olympiad and the World Pairs), two of only eight players ever to have done so. Marcelo is the only player ever to have won the World Pairs twice.

João Campos and Miguel Villas Boas are relatively new on the world scene. Both are in their early thirties but they have already achieved something I have not so far managed to do — they have reached the final of the Rosenblum Cup (in Lille in 1998, where they lost to the Italians).

The third pair, Roberto Mello and Ricardo Janz, are both experienced players who have been around a long time. They were members of the Brazilian squad that won the 1989 Bermuda Bowl in Perth, Australia.

The format for the quarter-final is six 16-board sets over two days.

Quarter-Final: Set One
Running Score: USA 0 — Brazil 0

Eric and I are sent into the Open Room to play North-South against João Campos and Miguel Villas Boas. These two youngsters have the talent level of Chagas-Branco but at the moment they lack the experience, which is very important at this level. I look for them to be bright stars in the future of Brazilian bridge.

The set starts quietly and then, at favorable vulnerability with West the dealer, we pick up:

♠ K 8   ♡ A K J 8 5 2   ◇ K Q 8   ♣ 6 5

It is rare these days that one gets to open with a strong **one club** in fourth seat, but that is exactly what happens. (It is even more unusual on a deal where, as it turns out, the opponents are cold for game!)

João Campos

Partner responds with a negative **one diamond** and we have another easy choice — **one heart**. West joins in with a **one spade** overcall, Eric raises to **two hearts**, and East bids **three clubs**, alerted and described as lead-directional with a spade fit.

Our hand has not been improved by West's spade overcall and although we have a sixth heart we are not worth a game try. If we pass now, though, West will surely convert to Three Spades. Competing to **three hearts** gives the opponents a chance to sell out, which is what we'd most like them to do.

The auction takes a curious turn now — West raises to Four Clubs and partner carries on to Four Hearts. A little surprisingly, there is no further bidding.

WEST	NORTH	EAST	SOUTH
V. Boas	*Eric*	*Campos*	*Us*
pass	pass	pass	1♣[1]
pass	1◊[2]	pass	1♡
1♠	2♡	3♣[3]	3♡
4♣	4♡	all pass	

1. Artificial, 16+.
2. Negative.
3. Lead-directing, with a spade fit.

West leads the four of clubs and dummy appears with:

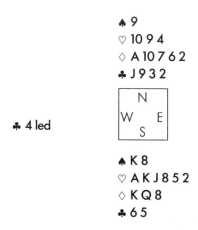

```
              ♠ 9
              ♡ 10 9 4
              ◊ A 10 7 6 2
              ♣ J 9 3 2
              ┌─────────┐
              │    N    │
   ♣ 4 led    │ W     E │
              │    S    │
              └─────────┘
              ♠ K 8
              ♡ A K J 8 5 2
              ◊ K Q 8
              ♣ 6 5
```

East wins the opening lead with the king of clubs, cashes the ace, and then switches to a spade. Our king loses to West's ace and the spade queen forces us to ruff in dummy.

The hands fit together well. Eric's judgement in bidding Four Hearts because he expected me to have fitting diamond values based on the opponents' bidding was spot on. Now all I have to do is guess the trumps.

A heart to the ace collects a low card from each defender and we return to dummy with the ace of diamonds. When dummy's final heart is led, East produces the last low trump. **Would you finesse or play for the drop?**

> Although the a priori percentages just about favor playing for the 2-2 break, the bidding suggests that this will be the wrong thing to do here. West's Four Clubs bid was fairly unusual. He will surely hold a pure hand for that action (i.e. most of his cards will be in the black suits), so a singleton heart is far more likely than a doubleton queen. I therefore take the finesse and claim my contract when West discards.

Ten tricks — plus 420. Teammates are expecting to lose IMPs on this deal as they also missed bidding Four Spades on the East-West cards — Chagas bought the hand in 3NT from the South seat. A club lead and spade switch put paid to his chances immediately, but a subsequent defensive slip let declarer score a sixth trick. No harm done, though — 11 IMPs to the good guys.

With E-W vulnerable, we then pick up:

♠ K 3　♡ A K 10 9　◇ J 10 5　♣ 8 7 6 3

Eric opens with a nebulous **one diamond** (10-15 HCP with no 5-card major but not a balanced 10-12 because we play a mini notrump in the first two seats non-vulnerable). RHO overcalls **one heart** and it's up to us. **Do you have any thoughts?**

> The first option is whether to play for a penalty by passing quickly, intending to pass partner's re-opening double. With only a four-card trump stack, this is a very dangerous strategy. I had a hand once, against Stansby-Martel, where I defended two diamonds doubled for minus 180 when we were cold for seven spades! I had only a four-card trump stack, and it's a lesson I will never forget.

Having decided that defending is not an option, the choice is between an invitational Two Notrump and a direct jump to game.

Because he has not opened a mini notrump, we know that Eric will have a full strength opening bid (12+ to 15) if he is balanced. He may be lighter if he is unbalanced, but then he will hold a potential source of tricks in one of the minors, either of which our holdings will help. Add in the extra value of the heart intermediates after the overcall and this hand is too good for an invitation. We therefore take the bull by the horns and leap directly to game — **three notrump**.

The auction has been brief:

WEST	NORTH	EAST	SOUTH
V- Boas	Eric	Campos	Us
	1◊[1]	1♡	3NT

all pass

1.   10-15, no 5-card major, at least 2 diamonds, but not 10-12 balanced.

West leads the six of spades and Eric's dummy is not very inspiring although his heart holding is a welcome sight:

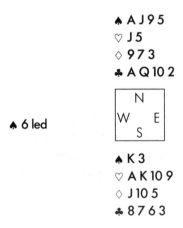

♠ A J 9 5
♡ J 5
◊ 9 7 3
♣ A Q 10 2

♠ 6 led

♠ K 3
♡ A K 10 9
◊ J 10 5
♣ 8 7 6 3

Assuming that the queen of hearts is onside, we can count seven tricks — four hearts, two spades and one club. It looks like West has led a long suit, so the jack of spades is probably worth a trick too. That's eight. A successful club finesse would give us nine tricks but East will surely hold the king of clubs to justify his overcall on such a poor heart suit. As soon as the defenders gain the lead, it will be obvious to switch to diamonds, enabling them to cash at least four tricks in that suit.

Do you have any thoughts?

The opponents are playing fourth-best leads, so the Rule of Eleven tells us that East holds one spade higher than the six. We therefore put in the nine of spades at Trick 1, and it holds.

That's the first hurdle overcome. Desperate times call for desperate measures, and it seems that the best way to divert the defenders' attention away from the diamond suit is for us to attack it. We therefore lead a low diamond from dummy at Trick 2. East follows with a low card, we play the jack, and West produces the six of diamonds. Now we can count nine tricks!

It is a simple matter to cash the king of spades, cross to the ace of clubs, cash the ace of spades, run the jack of hearts and repeat the heart hook. This is the full deal:

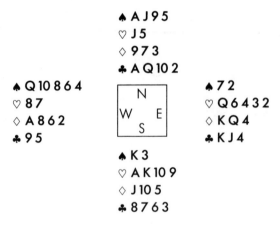

♠ A J 9 5
♡ J 5
◊ 9 7 3
♣ A Q 10 2

♠ Q 10 8 6 4
♡ 8 7
◊ A 8 6 2
♣ 9 5

♠ 7 2
♡ Q 6 4 3 2
◊ K Q 4
♣ K J 4

♠ K 3
♡ A K 10 9
◊ J 10 5
♣ 8 7 6 3

Obviously, playing a diamond worked much better than I dared hope. Once East failed to split his honors, though, the suit was blocked for the defenders, which was the real objective. If West had held the jack of clubs, then two finesses in that suit would have brought home the contract at that point.

The main purpose of playing a diamond was to block the suit if it were splitting 5-2. Suppose East held ◊ Kx — it would be far from obvious for him to rise with the king at Trick 2.

At the other table, after a similar auction, West led his partner's heart suit and declarer won in hand to take the club finesse. East won with the king of clubs and switched to diamonds, defeating the contract out of hand. When declarer eventually repeated the club finesse, the jack of clubs scored the sixth trick for the defense. Another 11 IMPs in the plus column.

The set finishes with a curious hand. There is an old adage that says, 'be wary of what you wish for, as you may get it'. One advantage of the Multi Two Diamonds opening is that the opponents sometimes cannot tell which suit you hold. Very occasionally, they even play in your Weak Two suit...

Vulnerable against not, we deal and pick up:

♠ A J 10 7 5   ♡ 7   ◇ A 10 7 5   ♣ 10 6 4

I have mentioned earlier our partnership philosophy when it comes to choosing between pass and a bid, particularly when first to speak; whenever possible, we prefer the positive action, vulnerability notwithstanding.

Our choices as dealer here are to pass, to open One Spade or to set the die rolling with a Weak Two via the Multi **two diamonds**. Having selected the latter option, the auction then takes a turn that must surely be good news... LHO overcalls **two spades**, which is passed back to us. We have nothing further to add, having apparently done enough damage already.

This is the full hand:

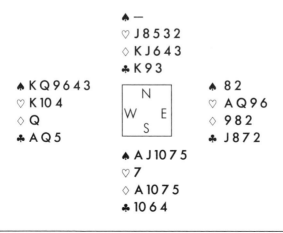

♠ —
♡ J 8 5 3 2
◇ K J 6 4 3
♣ K 9 3

♠ K Q 9 6 4 3
♡ K 10 4
◇ Q
♣ A Q 5

♠ 8 2
♡ A Q 9 6
◇ 9 8 2
♣ J 8 7 2

♠ A J 10 7 5
♡ 7
◇ A 10 7 5
♣ 10 6 4

It is all rather annoying. Rather than pushing the opponents into a poor contract, the effect of our preemptive opening has been to steer them into their best spot. Eric kicked off with a heart lead and we can take only five tricks. North-South -110 looks likely to be a good result for the Brazilians.

Miguel Villas-Boas

Left to their own devices, it is not easy for East-West to go plus on the deal, and our teammates did well to do so. After a pass from the Brazilian South, West opened One Spade and East responded One Notrump. West thought he was halfway between a Two Spade rebid and a jump to Three Spades. He thus temporized with Two Clubs, intending to continue with Three Hearts, describing his hand fairly well, if his partner gave preference back to Two Spades. Our East player judged well, though, by passing Two Clubs. Although this contract was not a thing of beauty, it had the merit of making eight tricks, holding the loss on the deal to a single IMP.

Both teams have played fairly well and, at the end of the opening stanza, we hold a 10-IMP lead.

Quarter-Final: Set Two
Running Score: USA 36 — Brazil 26

For the second set, our opponents are Roberto Mello and Ricardo Janz. Both are very experienced and excellent card players. They are a solid third pair for this team.

We are faced with a tough bidding problem on the very first board of the stanza. With both sides vulnerable, we deal and pick up:

♠ J 9 7 4   ♡ K 7   ◇ A K 5   ♣ A K J 10

Opening 2NT on 19 points is not something that is particularly desirable but we have found it necessary within the framework of our system. In fact, we open all 19-point hands with 2NT but most 21-counts with One Club. Our range for 2NT is therefore 19 to a bad 21. Although this hand is not a particularly meritorious 19-count, it falls comfortably within the range and we have to start with an opening **two notrump**.

Partner responds **three clubs**, asking for five-card majors, and our **three diamonds** denies one. Eric continues with **three hearts**, showing four spades, and our **three spades** confirms a fit in the suit. Then comes RKCB — **four notrump** — and we show our two key cards and deny the queen of spades with **five hearts**. Eric's next move is **six hearts**, which offers me a choice between slam in spades and notrump.

> We have built many 'choice of game' and 'choice of slam' bids into our system. Many pairs would probably treat bids such as Eric's Six Hearts here as some sort of grand slam try. Ideally, you want most bids available to investigate a grand slam but reserving one to offer a choice of six-level contracts is a useful tool. Having said that, you cannot afford misunderstandings at the six-level, and it takes a good partnership to have the confidence to know exactly which bids are 'choice of...' in various auctions.

Since you are fortunate enough to be armed with this useful toy, **which slam would you choose on this hand?**

There are plenty of reasons for choosing the notrump slam here. We have two four-card suits and, with the finesse, clubs will provide four tricks opposite as little as two low cards. When partner offers the choice of slams, he should have plenty of high card points for us. If he thought it was a 'thin slam', he would not offer the choice.

With the club ten but not the ten of spades, the choice is easy and our **six notrump** bid ends the auction.

WEST	NORTH	EAST	SOUTH
Mello	*Eric*	*Janz*	*Us*
			2NT
pass	3♣[1]	pass	3◇[2]
pass	3♡[3]	pass	3♠
pass	4NT[4]	pass	5♡[5]
pass	6♡[6]	pass	6NT
all pass			

1.   Asking for a 5-card major.
2.   Denying a 5-card major.
3.   Showing four spades
4.   RKCB
5.   Two key cards without the ♠Q.
6.   Offering a choice between spades and notrump.

West leads the eight of diamonds and Eric produces:

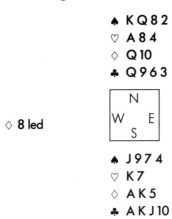

```
              ♠ K Q 8 2
              ♡ A 8 4
              ◇ Q 10
              ♣ Q 9 6 3
                  ┌─────────┐
                  │    N    │
  ◇ 8 led         │ W     E │
                  │    S    │
                  └─────────┘
              ♠ J 9 7 4
              ♡ K 7
              ◇ A K 5
              ♣ A K J 10
```

Eric did well to offer us a choice of slams. It is clear that 6NT is the best spot — six spades could be defeated by a ruff if the defender with the ace of spades holds either four clubs or a seven-card red suit, and six clubs may go down on a spade ruff.

Indeed, even without the risk of a ruff, notrump is better. All will be well if spades break 3-2 but if either defender holds ♠A10xx we will have to guess correctly. With spades as trumps, we would have to make that decision immediately. Playing in notrump, we have time to find out more about the hand before committing ourselves.

How would you approach the play?

It seems right to win the diamond lead in hand and to lead a spade to the king, which holds the trick. Now what?

Our next move is to see what clues the club suit holds and, when we cash two rounds, West discards a diamond. If anyone is short in spades, it is now very likely to be East. We play a diamond to the queen, just to untangle that suit, and play a low spade towards the jack. East's heart discard is a welcome sight!

It is now a simple matter to cash our twelve tricks, taking the proven finesse against West's ten of spades in the process.

Teammates were slightly worried about this board. They had held a five clubs contract to eleven tricks by leading the ace and a second round of spades for a ruff, and they are delighted to gain 13 IMPs on the deal.

To even things up and to prove that it is impossible to judge what might happen at the other table, a few boards later we produce a result that is rather inferior to the one for which teammates were hoping. With neither side vulnerable, we deal and pick up:

♠ A K 9 7 ♡ A K 5 2 ◇ K ♣ A K 10 5

We have an easy first bid — a strong and artificial **one club**. LHO enters the fray with a weak jump overcall of **two hearts** and partner **doubles**, showing a balanced hand with 8+ HCP or any hand in the 6-7 HCP range. **What would you do?**

It seems clear to pass the double since any other action is likely to lead to playing a non-vulnerable 3NT for plus 400. The penalty from two hearts, if partner has the balanced hand, could be substantially more than that.

Whether we try to punish opponents who interfere over our Big Club or just ignore them and aim for our best spot depends to some extent on what methods they use. Our general style, though, is to try to penalize. We want opponents to know that we will readily double and defend, and we accept that we will sometimes lose IMPs trying to punish them. Particularly, we aim to penalize those pairs who adopt a 'bid over a Strong Club on anything' approach.

On this board, things do not go quite as planned, though. This is the full deal:

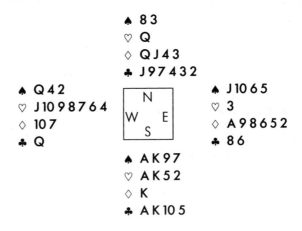

```
              ♠ 8 3
              ♡ Q
              ◇ Q J 4 3
              ♣ J 9 7 4 3 2
♠ Q 4 2                        ♠ J 10 6 5
♡ J 10 9 8 7 6 4      N        ♡ 3
◇ 10 7            W       E    ◇ A 9 8 6 5 2
♣ Q                   S        ♣ 8 6
              ♠ A K 9 7
              ♡ A K 5 2
              ◇ K
              ♣ A K 10 5
```

Eric leads a spade and we play three rounds of the suit, but his ruff is with a natural trump trick. Worse still is that declarer's diamond loser can now be discarded on dummy's fourth spade while we impotently follow suit. We make just one club and our two high hearts to defeat the contract by a trick. North-South plus 100.

Having conceded minus 520, our teammates had fully expected to gain on this deal. It is, after all, a very easy slam to bid, with plenty of top tricks and nothing to the play. You can be sure the Brazilian North-South pair were delighted to gain 9 IMPs for their poor effort.

In retrospect, I think that passing the double of two hearts is simply a really bad bid! If you imagine LHO with ♡ QJ10xxx, then defending is virtually certain to be wrong, no matter what the rest of the hand. The best case scenario is probably plus 500 when we can make plus 460 by declaring. I think it is correct to jump to 3NT (2NT would be non-forcing). This wouldn't get us to slam on the actual layout, but it would have saved us 9 IMPs. This deal once again illustrates the danger of playing for a low-level penalty when you hold only four trumps.

It is sometimes hard to tell what your objective is on a hand. If you have lots of high cards, you do not usually look upon a minus score as a good thing. It can be, though. What are your thoughts when you pick up this collection with neither side vulnerable?

♠ Q ♡ A3 ◇ AKQJ9 ♣ K10854

The hand has potential but you are put immediately under pressure when your RHO opens **three spades**.

What do you plan to do now?

Anything could be right. This is the sort of problem that is regularly presented to bidding panels in magazines around the world, and there is no right or wrong answer. It's just a matter of guessing what will work on this particular deal.

Does partner hold ♠ KJx, when 3NT is right? Does he have long hearts, when double will work best? Does he have a good fit for one of the minors, when Four Notrump (or Four Spades) is the winning choice?

The one bid that is not in the game is a Four Diamonds overcall. You must take a position when you are cornered like this, and Three Notrump, Double and Four Notrump are the clearest choices.

We guess to bid **three notrump** and everyone passes. West leads the king of hearts and when partner puts down a one-count with two small spades it does not seem like good news. However, although we had not intended 3NT as a sacrifice when we made the bid, that is how things work out since the full hand looks like this:

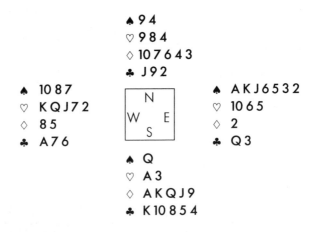

	♠ 9 4	
	♡ 9 8 4	
	◊ 10 7 6 4 3	
	♣ J 9 2	
♠ 10 8 7		♠ A K J 6 5 3 2
♡ K Q J 7 2	N	♡ 10 6 5
◊ 8 5	W E	◊ 2
♣ A 7 6	S	♣ Q 3
	♠ Q	
	♡ A 3	
	◊ A K Q J 9	
	♣ K 10 8 5 4	

We take the opening lead with the ace of hearts and cash five diamond tricks. The defenders claim the rest as soon as they get in, but minus 150 is a good result.

At the other table, East opened Four Spades and the Brazilian with our hand came in with an unusual 4NT. West bid Five Spades and there matters rested. Not unreasonably, South did not find the opening lead of the nine of diamonds (for North to overtake and switch to a club through the queen). So, our teammates chalked up plus 450 and we gain an unlikely 7 IMPs on the deal.

We win the second stanza by 19 IMPs, 44-25, to lead by 29 with a third of the match played.

At the Beijing Zoo

We all decide that Eric and I should take a rest for the final set of the day. The general plan is that we will play one or two sets tomorrow if things continue to go well. With luck, we will be well rested when the semifinal starts, whereas our opponents will have struggled through their quarter-final.

I meet up with Shirlee and set off for a relaxing meal, having agreed to meet Eric back at the hotel in time for the scoring. We find our way to the center of Beijing and into a tiny restaurant in one of the dingy back streets. Dinner is fabulous and we are in good spirits as we head out to the hotel. The first inkling that things have not gone well comes when I see a beaming Gabriel Chagas surrounded by a large group of noisy, backslapping Brazilians in the far corner of the lobby. I make my way quickly up the stairs to the area where we have been meeting to score and the downcast faces there confirm my first impressions.

Eric is there and so too is one of our pairs. I am greeted with the news that they have three disasters and nothing much in the potential plus column. Ten minutes later, our second pair join us and the looks on their faces confirm that the scoring is not going to be a pleasant experience. When the dust clears, we have lost the set 56-9. Not only has our lead completely gone, we are now 18 IMPs behind. The good news, though, is that we still have half of the match left. I suspect that Eric and I will be required for all three sets tomorrow. Any thoughts of going into the semifinal rested are out of the window. What's important now is to make sure we go into the semifinal at all. The battle has been well and truly joined.

In the other quarter-finals, Canada is almost 100 IMPs ahead against South Africa, while Poland holds a handy 45-IMP lead against China. The other match is even closer than ours, with the Swedes leading the reigning Olympiad champions, France, by just 2 IMPs at the halfway stage.

We start as we did yesterday, in the Open Room against Campos and Villas Boas. With neither side vulnerable and Eric the dealer, we pick up:

♠ A 5　♡ J 9 4　◇ K Q 10 8 6 4 3　♣ 7

Eric opens **one heart** (5-card major and 10-15 HCP) and rightie passes.

Any thoughts?

There is a wide variety of hands on which our style is to raise a major-suit opening directly to game. The common theme is that we have no slam interest. Facing an opening bid limited to 15 HCP, slam is not impossible with this 10-count, but it requires partner to hold the 'magic' hand — something like ♡AKQxx and the ◇A. (And even then the opponents may have a cheap save at the seven-level.)

The tactical advantages of bidding Four Hearts directly outweigh the small risk of finding partner with the perfect hand for slam. We are prepared to suffer a loss when he has a 'perfecto' in order to get to what is likely to be our best contract (game in partner's major) as quickly as possible.

The objective is to exert maximum pressure on the opponents without giving them much information on which to base their decision. A fair proportion of the time, this will be our hand and we will be able to make ten tricks in hearts. However, the odds that the opponents belong in spades or even clubs, either because they can make game or because it's a good save, are high enough to make the preemptive action a big winner in the long run.

What's more, bidding four-of-a-major directly makes it very dangerous for the opponents to compete, especially when the raiser may have only three-card trump support, as we often do. Opponents frequently enter the auction at a high level expecting a guaranteed fit, only to find to their considerable cost that they do not have one.

We therefore jump directly to **four hearts**. Today, LHO refuses to be shut out, and Villas-Boas comes in with a **four spade** overcall. Eric carries on to **five hearts** and Campos raises to **five spades**.

How do you rate your hand now?

When Eric bids Five Hearts, we can expect him to hold extra heart length or spade shortage, and probably both. He is also bidding it to make, otherwise he would pass Four Spades around to us. A pass from us now would not be forcing, as we could have had a very weak hand for our initial raise. We must do something to show strength in order to protect our equity on the deal. The odds are still that we cannot make slam, so the only alternative is a **double**.

Thus ends an exciting auction:

WEST	NORTH	EAST	SOUTH
V-Boas	Eric	Campos	Us
	1♡	pass	4♡
4♠	5♡	5♠	dbl
all pass			

The full hand looks like this:

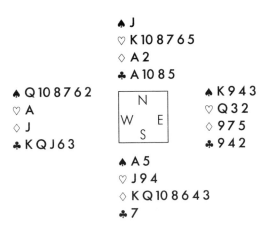

```
              ♠ J
              ♡ K 10 8 7 6 5
              ◊ A 2
              ♣ A 10 8 5
♠ Q 10 8 7 6 2           ♠ K 9 4 3
♡ A                      ♡ Q 3 2
◊ J                      ◊ 9 7 5
♣ K Q J 6 3             ♣ 9 4 2
              ♠ A 5
              ♡ J 9 4
              ◊ K Q 10 8 6 4 3
              ♣ 7
```

Eric leads a heart around to the ace and declarer immediately plays a spade to the jack, king and our ace. The club switch is not difficult to find and we quickly score our ruff. The ace of diamonds is the fourth and last trick for the defense. North-South plus 300 and a flat board.

After three dull boards, with partner again the dealer but this time at favorable vulnerability, we pick up:

♠ 10 8 5 3 2   ♡ —   ◊ Q J 9 6   ♣ A 9 6 5

Eric opens proceedings with **one spade** and RHO passes. As you may have guessed from the previous deal, our style is to deny the opponents a chance to come in cheaply, so any thoughts of a splinter in case partner has the right cards for slam can be ignored. We jump directly to **four spades** but Villas-Boas is having none of it — he comes in with a **double**. Partner passes and RHO removes to **five hearts**.

What are your thoughts?

We have all been told often in recent years that 'the five-level belongs to the opponents'. Even so, there are exceptions to every rule. Is this one of them?

There is no guarantee that Five Spades will be a successful bid, but a void in their suit is an exceptional holding, and one that it is hard for partner to visualize. A void in the opponents' suit usually means it is right to 'take the push' to the next level. Not always, but the odds favor it. On this particular hand, our minor-suit holdings suggest that we may have some defense against Five Hearts, so this is a particularly close problem. We don't much like bidding Five Spades, but we think it's just about the percentage action. We push on to **five spades**, to which leftie applies a **double**.

WEST	NORTH	EAST	SOUTH
V-Boas	*Eric*	*Campos*	*us*
	1♠	pass	4♠
dbl	pass	5♡	5♠
dbl	all pass		

The full deal looks like this:

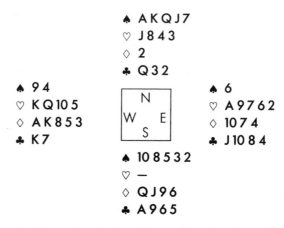

```
                    ♠ A K Q J 7
                    ♡ J 8 4 3
                    ◇ 2
                    ♣ Q 3 2
    ♠ 9 4                          ♠ 6
    ♡ K Q 10 5                     ♡ A 9 7 6 2
    ◇ A K 8 5 3                    ◇ 10 7 4
    ♣ K 7                          ♣ J 10 8 4
                    ♠ 10 8 5 3 2
                    ♡ —
                    ◇ Q J 9 6
                    ♣ A 9 6 5
```

East leads the jack of clubs, ducked to the king. West cashes the king of diamonds and although it seems likely that it is declarer who holds the singleton, he has little option but to try cashing the ace too. Not today — Eric ruffs and is soon claiming eleven tricks. North-South plus 650 and 5 IMPs in when teammates allow Chagas-Branco to play peacefully in four spades.

Thanks to West's double, pressing on to five spades has turned out to be the best decision. We could have collected plus 500 against five hearts, though. Not that partner would have doubled if we had passed it around to him — we actually have to double it ourselves in order to beat par legitimately on the deal.

That's too tough!

We seem to be getting slightly the better of the exchanges in this set. With both sides vulnerable towards the end of the stanza, RHO deals this promising collection to us:

♠ A Q 10 8   ♡ K J 2   ◇ A 3   ♣ A 9 5 4

Campos opens **one heart** and we must decide whether this hand falls into the range for a 15-18 HCP One Notrump overcall.

With a presumed double stopper in hearts and such a good hand for the other major, I consider this hand an easy upgrade to a 19-count. With just ♡Kxx and the jack elsewhere, I would overcall One Notrump.

(At favorable vulnerability, we play a comic, or Gardiner, 1NT overcall in WBF events — it has been banned in the US as it is deemed to be destructive. This would have no effect on whether a strong hand qualified for a One Notrump overcall, though.)

We elect to start with a takeout **double**. LHO bids **one spade** and partner competes with **two diamonds**.

Our style is that a takeout double, unless we are very strong, guarantees at least three-card support for any unbid major but may have only a doubleton in an unbid minor. The classic reason for this is that, with 4-4-2-3 shape and decent values, you have to be able to make a takeout double of a One Club opening bid.

After a pass from opener, we must now decide whether this hand is good enough to take a shot at game.

What can we expect from partner for his Two Diamonds bid? Had LHO passed my double, he would have been forced to bid Two Diamonds on any hand, so Two Notrump would now have described this hand fairly accurately. For a free bid, particularly in a minor for which there is no guarantee of real support, I would expect him to hold fair values and a decent suit. We also play that a jump to Three Diamonds in competition is preemptive, so he cannot hold a weak hand with long diamonds.

Facing a 6-7 count with five decent diamonds, we do not want to stop short of game, and **three notrump** is the obvious choice. LHO's Double suggests that perhaps we have overestimated our combined assets but there is nothing we can do about that now.

WEST	NORTH	EAST	SOUTH
V-Boas	*Eric*	*Campos*	*Us*
		1♡	dbl
1♠	2◇	pass	3NT
dbl	all pass		

West leads the ♡4 and Eric produces a surprisingly good dummy in the circumstances:

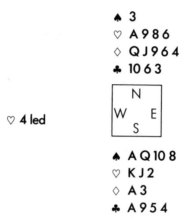

```
            ♠ 3
            ♡ A 9 8 6
            ◇ Q J 9 6 4
            ♣ 10 6 3
         ┌─────────┐
         │    N    │
♡ 4 led  │ W     E │
         │    S    │
         └─────────┘
            ♠ A Q 10 8
            ♡ K J 2
            ◇ A 3
            ♣ A 9 5 4
```

Dummy's nine of hearts fetches the queen and we win with the king. We have little option but to go after diamonds, so we immediately play the ace and a second round towards dummy.

In this type of situation, vulnerable and doubled, you should definitely be thinking of making your contract, with down one the worst case scenario. If you can hold it to down one and your teammates go plus, you will suffer only a small loss.

What inferences can we draw from West's double? I think the opponents' high card points are divided either 4-11 or 5-10 (West must have something for his double). Can we infer anything about his diamond holding? It's hard to know exactly, but I feel the double is based more on points and also that he is taking a bit of a shot.

When West follows with a low diamond on the second round, should we consider playing the nine?

It's a possible play, but a big one. And it is one that I would never make in this type of high-risk situation. Should the ◇9 lose to the ten, it would be a huge disaster.

We put up the queen of diamonds, which loses to the king, and East switches to the queen of clubs. If diamonds are going to break, there will be no problem. If they are not, then we will have to scratch around for tricks elsewhere. It cannot hurt us that the defenders are attacking a suit we would otherwise have to broach and, as we would not object to a club continuation, a smooth duck seems right. Nevertheless, East switches to the ♠7 next. We would prefer not to lose another quick trick, so the queen seems like the right spade to try. Sure enough, that holds.

We can count eight tricks now without any long diamonds — three hearts, two spades, two diamonds and a club. If we can set up a second club trick, we will be home. We therefore try the ace of clubs next and this drops West's king. Our nine and ten of clubs are now equals against East's jack and it is a simple matter to set up our ninth trick: North-South plus 750.

This is the full deal:

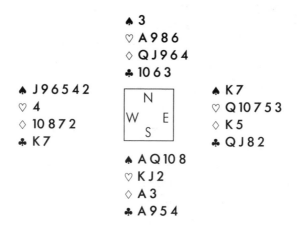

```
              ♠ 3
              ♡ A 9 8 6
              ◇ Q J 9 6 4
              ♣ 10 6 3
♠ J 9 6 5 4 2           ♠ K 7
♡ 4             N       ♡ Q 10 7 5 3
◇ 10 8 7 2    W   E     ◇ K 5
♣ K 7            S      ♣ Q J 8 2
              ♠ A Q 10 8
              ♡ K J 2
              ◇ A 3
              ♣ A 9 5 4
```

Curiously, the heart lead does not seem to give us anything that we couldn't do ourselves, although entries to dummy are limited and we need to finesse in both majors as well as set up tricks in both minors. The defenders here were just too active, although the contract can always be made, even after misguessing in diamonds.

At the other table, the defenders attacked spades at every opportunity, setting up a winner there. Declarer was left to play clubs himself and finished a trick short: 13 IMPs to the good guys.

The final deal of the set arrives and with the opponents only vulnerable we are dealt one of my normal rubber bridge hands:

♠ J 6   ♡ 9 6 2   ◇ 9 4 3   ♣ 10 9 6 3 2

Eric opens **one diamond** and RHO passes.

Any thoughts?

I don't psyche often — I don't believe it's a good thing for experts to do against weaker opponents. But it's a legitimate tactic against opponents who are capable of looking after themselves and I couldn't resist it on this hand.

Opposite a 10-15 HCP One Diamond opening, the opponents are likely to be cold for game, and perhaps even slam. At favorable vulnerability the risks of responding in a short major are outweighed by the potential gains. Of course, this type of psyche is much safer playing a Strong Club system than it would be playing Standard, but it is still far from risk-free. If the bidding gets competitive, a disaster could easily occur.

Having decided to bid, which major should we choose? One Heart is slightly safer, but there are two reasons for preferring spades. Firstly, **one spade** is slightly more preemptive. Secondly, it's more likely that spades is the opponents' best suit.

LHO passes and Eric rebids **two diamonds**. We have done enough, but Villas-Boas is not to be denied — he jumps to **three spades**, which Campos raises to **four spades**.

WEST	**NORTH**	**EAST**	**SOUTH**
V-Boas	_Eric_	_Campos_	_Us_
	1◇	pass	1♠
pass	2◇	pass	pass
3♠	pass	4♠	all pass

Our decision to respond in spades has worked particularly well as it robbed the Brazilians of the space to investigate the hand fully. This turns out to be the full deal:

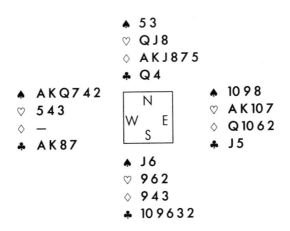

```
                   ♠ 5 3
                   ♡ Q J 8
                   ◇ A K J 8 7 5
                   ♣ Q 4
   ♠ A K Q 7 4 2        ┌───────┐        ♠ 10 9 8
   ♡ 5 4 3              │   N   │        ♡ A K 10 7
   ◇ —               W  │       │  E     ◇ Q 10 6 2
   ♣ A K 8 7            │   S   │        ♣ J 5
                        └───────┘
                   ♠ J 6
                   ♡ 9 6 2
                   ◇ 9 4 3
                   ♣ 10 9 6 3 2
```

Declarer scores all thirteen tricks with the aid of the double heart finesse: East-West plus 710.

Since they also missed the slam, our teammates are delighted to win IMPs on this deal, but this comes about in a curious fashion. North chose to open an off-center 14-16 1NT against them, and South tried Stayman. West doubled to show a good hand with some clubs which North, quite remarkably, passed. Not unreasonably, so did both East and South. Declarer managed to score four tricks, so that was only plus 800. Normally, this would be a poor exchange when a vulnerable slam was available, but a 3-IMP gain as things turn out. Curiously, at the sixteen tables where this board was played (eight in the four Bermuda Bowl quarter-finals and eight in the Venice Cup), the slam was bid only once!

We win the highest-scoring set of boards so far by 50-25 to retake the lead by 7 IMPs. There are 32 deals remaining.

We are back in the Open Room for the fifth set, and for the first time in the match we are head-to-head with Brazil's anchor pair, Gabriel Chagas and Marcelo Branco. Both are extremely talented players with a wealth of experience. They are also highly imaginative and intuitive players, which makes them very dangerous opponents.

On the second board of the stanza, at favorable vulnerability and with Branco, on our right, the dealer, we pick up this monster:

♠ A K 10 7 2   ♡ —   ◇ A Q J 7 6 5   ♣ A K

Marcelo passes and our first move is easy — a strong and artificial **one club**. With the vulnerable opponents silent, we have this auction to ourselves.

Partner responds with a negative **one diamond**. Our style is to bid majors before minors, so we continue with **one spade**, forcing, which although it guarantees only a four-card suit also promises an unbalanced hand. Eric's **one notrump** now shows 0-5 HCP without four spades.

We want to insist on game, so our next move is a jump to **three diamonds**, showing at least a five-card suit. Eric gives preference to **three spades** and we continue with a **four club** cuebid. Eric makes the most discouraging noise available to him — **four spades**. **Do you think we are worth one more effort?**

If Eric has as little as ♠Qxx, we want to play in slam, and we can get that information via Blackwood — **four notrump**. As expected, Eric denies a key card with **five clubs**, and our **five diamonds** now asks about the spade queen. When he denies that card with **five hearts**, it is time to give up, so we sign off in **five spades** and hope that we are not already too high.

This has been the auction:

WEST	NORTH	EAST	SOUTH
Chagas	Eric	Branco	Us
		pass	1♣[1]
pass	1◊[2]	pass	1♠
pass	1NT[3]	pass	3◊
pass	3♠	pass	4♣[4]
pass	4♠	pass	4NT[5]
pass	5♣[6]	pass	5◊[7]
pass	5♡[8]	pass	5♠
all pass			

1. Artificial 16+.
2. Negative.
3. 0-5, without four spades.
4. Cuebid.
5. RKCB.
6. Key cards, 0 or 3.
7. Queen ask.
8. No spade queen.

Chagas leads the ace of hearts and this is the dummy:

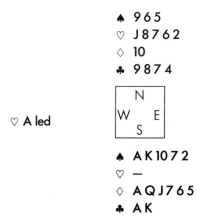

```
              ♠ 9 6 5
              ♡ J 8 7 6 2
              ◊ 10
              ♣ 9 8 7 4
                  N
  ♡ A led      W     E
                  S
              ♠ A K 10 7 2
              ♡ —
              ◊ A Q J 7 6 5
              ♣ A K
```

There is a lot of work to do here. We not only have to establish the diamonds, but we must also retain trump control and we have been forced at Trick 1.

We have to start diamonds straight away, so we cash the ◊A, ruff a diamond, and play a spade to the ace on which West follows with the jack. We lead the queen of diamonds next and West follows with the last low one. **Decision time** — should we ruff, playing for diamonds to break 3-3, or did West begin with ◊Kxxx?

Besides the technical merits of the two options, there is also an interesting psychological aspect to the problem. The opponents play upside-down count signals on declarer's lead — Chagas, on my left, has given a high-low signal to show an odd number of diamonds, while Branco has followed upwards to show an even number. **Which of them is lying?**

Gabriel Chagas

Trumps may be breaking 3-2 but the odds strongly favor the jack's being a singleton. If that is the case, then it is more likely that the diamonds will break 4-2. Clearly, it is the defender who holds the king who has lied about his length in the suit, but which of them is that? My gut instinct says that the man with the king is more likely to follow suit without showing his length, whereas his partner, not realizing that there is a guess in the suit, is giving an honest signal. If that is the case, it will be Chagas who holds the diamond king, which backs up the technical argument of playing for the suit to split 4-2.

We discard a heart on the diamond queen and East ruffs. His heart return reduces our trump length again, but with East ruffing diamonds we can stay a step ahead. We ruff the fourth round of diamonds with dummy's nine of spades and East overruffs with the queen, but that's the end of the road for the defense. We ruff the third round of hearts with the ten of spades, draw the last trump with the king, and claim the remaining tricks with our minor-suit winners.

This is the full deal:

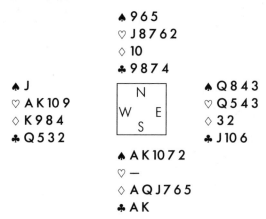

```
                    ♠ 9 6 5
                    ♡ J 8 7 6 2
                    ◇ 10
                    ♣ 9 8 7 4
♠ J                                    ♠ Q 8 4 3
♡ A K 10 9          N                  ♡ Q 5 4 3
◇ K 9 8 4       W       E              ◇ 3 2
♣ Q 5 3 2           S                  ♣ J 10 6
                    ♠ A K 10 7 2
                    ♡ —
                    ◇ A Q J 7 6 5
                    ♣ A K
```

As the cards lie, the defenders cannot legitimately defeat the contract once we have guessed the diamonds correctly. However, Branco could have put us to one more test. When he ruffed the third round of diamonds, his best chance was to return the eight of spades, forcing us to guess the trumps. We would have guessed right, though, wouldn't we?

We gain an IMP on this deal as the opponents in the other room stop in game and play safely for ten tricks.

After a run of fairly dull deals, we pick up:

♠ A 9 3   ♡ A K 10 7   ◇ K 9 7 2   ♣ 7 6

At unfavorable vulnerability, we play a 14-16 **one notrump** and this hand fits the bill. Partner raises to **three notrump** and West leads an attitude-style two of spades.

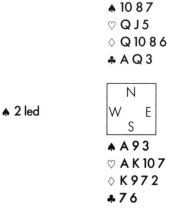

```
                    ♠ 10 8 7
                    ♡ Q J 5
                    ◇ Q 10 8 6
                    ♣ A Q 3
                        N
♠ 2 led         W       E
                        S
                    ♠ A 9 3
                    ♡ A K 10 7
                    ◇ K 9 7 2
                    ♣ 7 6
```

The lead sets up at least three spade tricks for the defense. We will also have to lose the ace of diamonds, so this contract is likely to come down to finding the diamond jack.

The opponents are playing attitude leads, so the chances are that the spades are splitting 5-2. We allow East to win the jack of spades at Trick 1 and he returns the ♠6. We could duck the second spade, guarding against a 4-3 spade break and aiming to play East for the ace of diamonds and intending to take the finesse against the diamond jack into his safe hand too.

This would be a mistake, though, as Chagas is certainly up to winning the second round of spades and finding a club switch, which would be most unwelcome. If the club king is offside, we could then go down even if we guess the diamonds correctly.

Have you decided which defender you would play to hold the jack of diamonds yet?

Since West appears to hold at least four spades, and thus a maximum of nine non-spades, the Theory of Vacant Spaces suggests that East is a slight favorite to hold any specific missing card — in this case, the jack of diamonds.

On the other hand, if spades are 5-2, then it must be right to finesse into the safe East hand. There is also a more significant piece of information that we have not yet taken into account. If spades are 4-3, then we can reasonably assume that West has led his longest suit. He is therefore more likely to hold three (or even four) diamonds than two. If West holds the diamond length, it is he and not East who is more likely to hold a specific diamond — i.e. the jack. All in all, it seems right to take the finesse for the jack of diamonds through West.

We cross to dummy in hearts to lead the first round of diamonds towards the king, just in case East was dealt ◇A-J doubleton, but he follows low and our king loses to the ace. West cashes his spades (they break 4-3) and exits with a club. We put up the ace, cash our heart winners and run the nine of diamonds.

When that loses to the jack, East cashes the king of clubs for two down. They say that a little learning is a dangerous thing but, believe me, sometimes a lot is too. At the other table, declarer guesses diamonds after the same opening lead so that's 13 IMPs out.

> It is vital that you take each result as it comes, although this is not always easy after you have made a losing decision. But it's 'water over the dam'. You must be ready to play the next hand without previous result(s) affecting your thinking or your concentration. Easier said than done, but essential if you are to be a regular winner.

We lose a low-scoring set 18-24. With sixteen deals remaining, we still lead, but by the slenderest of margins.

Marcelo Branco

Quarter-Final: Set Six
Running Score: USA 157 — Brazil 156

For the final stanza, we are in the Closed Room against Ricardo Janz and Roberto Mello. Early in the set, with only our side vulnerable, we pick up this promising collection:

♠ J ♡ A K J 9 7 ◇ Q J 10 7 2 ♣ K 2

After a pass on our left, Eric opens **one spade** and RHO comes in with a **two diamonds** overcall. **How do you feel about our hand now?**

The choices are to advance towards a vulnerable game with Two Hearts or to pass and play for a penalty, hoping that partner can reopen with a double. Fortunately, we are playing with screens so we do not have to make an instantaneous decision. Without screens, if we were going to pass it would be essential to do so in tempo to avoid embarrassing partner. **What would you do?**

I've already mentioned the dangers of playing for a penalty when holding only four trumps. Doing so when holding five trumps is a much more attractive proposition, even at unfavorable vulnerability. It is a much tougher decision at matchpoints, but at IMPs I don't mind taking a small loss if we collect 500 against a vulnerable game. The payoff is the big pick-up every time we get 300 or 500 when we cannot make game, which will frequently be the case. One major plus to playing a Strong Club system is that partner is limited when he opens something other than One Club. Although we would always bid game with this hand facing an opening bid, there is no certainty that it will make. For one thing, there is no guarantee that we even have a fit.

In these situations, IMPs are very similar to rubber bridge, and my vote is always to take the cash.

So, we elect to pass. Leftie passes and so too does partner. **How do you feel now?**

I recall feeling terrible at the time!

This is the full deal:

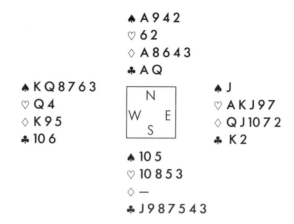

```
              ♠ A 9 4 2
              ♡ 6 2
              ◇ A 8 6 4 3
              ♣ A Q
♠ K Q 8 7 6 3        ┌───────┐        ♠ J
♡ Q 4                │   N   │        ♡ A K J 9 7
◇ K 9 5              │ W   E │        ◇ Q J 10 7 2
♣ 10 6               │   S   │        ♣ K 2
                     └───────┘
              ♠ 10 5
              ♡ 10 8 5 3
              ◇ —
              ♣ J 9 8 7 5 4 3
```

Our style is to reopen whenever we are short in the overcaller's suit, but with ◇Kxx there was no reason for Eric to double here. The contract drifts four down and the 7-2 club break means that we can make 3NT, although it is not a thing of beauty. Plus 200 East-West does not rate to be good, and I confess that it rather irks me to think that North will gain IMPs for this particularly disgusting overcall.

Paul Soloway

However, strange things can happen, and this is rather an unusual deal. Unless you are Victor Mollo's Rueful Rabbit, it is seldom good news when your side plays in the same suit at both tables. This deal was no exception. In the replay, there was no overcall from North. The Brazilian East-West identified the club weakness for notrump and then had a bidding misunderstanding to reach the dizzy heights of Six Diamonds!

Our North expressed his opinion about the chances of this contract succeeding in the traditional way. He was rather disappointed to get only his three aces, but that was still plus 500 and 12 IMPs in.

Midway through the set, again at unfavorable vulnerability, we deal and pick up:

♠ Q J 6 3   ♡ A Q 9 3   ◊ 7 6 4   ♣ 9 3

After two passes, Eric opens with a nebulous **one diamond** in third seat, and RHO makes a takeout **double**. We play transfers here, so we start with a **redouble**, showing at least four hearts. Roberto Mello, on our left, bids 1NT and partner competes to **two hearts**. We have nothing more to say but things have not finished yet. Mello reopens with a double, suggesting a maximum for his earlier 1NT, partner passes, and RHO bids Two Notrump. **Do you let this go or are you feeling aggressive?**

Our third-seat openings can be quite light non-vulnerable, but I expect a vulnerable One Diamond to be at least close to a genuine opening hand. Eric's Two Hearts tells us little, though, as he would make that bid on almost all hands containing four-card support.

Personally, I am not very aggressive when it comes to doubling partscores at IMPs. The risk-reward ratio is very low, plus it is a psychological blow if they make their contract.

Despite the foregoing, we elect to double and that concludes an eventful auction.

Looking back on it now, I am really surprised that I doubled Two Notrump. All I can say is that I must have been in a bad mood!

WEST	NORTH	EAST	SOUTH
Eric	Janz	Us	Mello
		pass	pass
1◇[1]	dbl	redbl[2]	1NT
2♡	pass	pass	dbl
pass	2NT	dbl	all pass

1. 10-15, at least two diamonds, no five-card major.
2. Transfer to hearts.

Eric leads the jack of hearts and this dummy comes down:

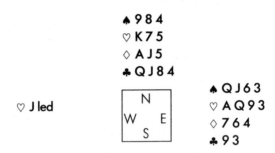

```
            ♠ 9 8 4
            ♡ K 7 5
            ◇ A J 5
            ♣ Q J 8 4
                        ♠ Q J 6 3
  ♡ J led                ♡ A Q 9 3
          ┌─────────┐   ◇ 7 6 4
          │    N    │   ♣ 9 3
          │ W     E │
          │    S    │
          └─────────┘
```

Declarer puts up the king of hearts and we win with the ace.

How do you think we should proceed?

We could cash our heart tricks but is there any rush to do so?

South has announced a diamond stopper so there is no future for us there and dummy's clubs look fairly robust. Spades is the obvious suit to attack and we should do so now in case we need our hearts as entries. For example, perhaps partner has a spade holding such as ♠A10x. Sure, we could lead the queen now, but that will not be a success if partner's spades are the doubleton king-ten.

We switch to a low spade and partner wins with the king. Declarer captures our jack on the second round and runs the ten of diamonds. Partner's diamond king appears on the next round and declarer cashes five tricks in the suit. When he leads a club, though, partner takes the ace and we can claim the remaining tricks in the majors. East-West plus 300 is worth 4 IMPs when teammates concede 140 to a heart partial.

Little happens in the remaining boards at our table and, although it feels as if we have had slightly the better of things, it would be a brave man who would bet on the outcome.

We walk down to the Vugraph Theater to find the penultimate deal being played in the Open Room. We are ahead by 5 IMPs and we watch our teammates bid agonizingly slowly to a game that will push the board. They reach game and, although the play seems to take forever, declarer is never in any real danger of going down.

I absolutely hate to watch Vugraph when my own team is playing. The last time I watched a whole set was during the final of the 1988 Olympiad in Venice, and I couldn't stand it! To watch the number of IMPs hanging in the balance on every bid and play was agonizing. After that experience, I don't even like to go into the Vugraph Theater to check the score when we are sitting out.

The final deal appears on the screen. The commentators announce to raucous cheers from the American contingent in the large audience that in the Closed Room we took a save for minus 500 against what looks like an easy vulnerable game. It is hard to see how we can lose IMPs on the deal, but stranger things have happened.

Things pass off peacefully today, though. In fact, the Brazilians allow our teammates to buy the hand in game and they score up plus 620 to register another 3-IMP gain.

We have survived a real nail-biter to win by 8 IMPs (198-190). We will celebrate with a few drinks tonight as there is no morning session tomorrow. Play in the semifinal starts at 2 p.m.

In the other quarter-finals, Canada's match against the South Africans was all but over at the halfway point and the Canucks win by a distance. Poland holds off a late rally from the Chinese and wins by 22 IMPs. The Swedes had led narrowly going into the last set against France, but a big final set from Chemla-Perron sees the French come through.

As owners of the best record in the Round Robin, the Canadians have the right to choose their semifinal opponents and they select the Poles. That leaves us to do battle with France, an opponent with whom we have had some epic encounters over the years. Both semifinals will be North America against Europe for a place in the Bermuda Bowl Final.

Brazil plays Poland on Uugraph

3

The Semifinal

The French are familiar foes. We beat them in the 1995 semifinal but lost to them in the 1992 Olympiad final and in the final of the 1997 Bermuda Bowl in Hammamet, Tunisia. They have won their share of World Championships and they will not be an easy team to beat. All three pairs play a very simple system and perhaps that is where our biggest edge lies, as they are all adept card players.

Paul Chemla is a living legend in France, and a larger-than-life character. Despite his reputation for abusing partners, his partnership with Michel Perron seems to work well.

Alain Levy and Christian Mari are both quiet, unassuming people away from the table, but they are fierce competitors. Both were members of the French team that won back-to-back World Team Olympiads in 1992 and 1996 followed by the Bermuda Bowl in 1997.

Franck Multon and Herve Mouiel can hardly be considered a 'third pair'. Mouiel was part of all three French World Championship teams and Multon was on the last two.

The format for the semifinal is the same as for the quarterfinal — six 16-board sets over two days.

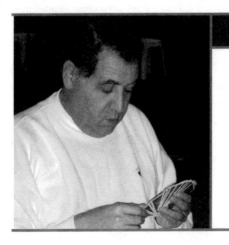

Paul Chemla

We played all three sets in the quarterfinal yesterday, so Eric and I get the first semifinal session off. If we are going to sit out, I much prefer to do it early and the first set of a fairly long match is the ideal time for us to take a breather. That way, if we are behind when we come in, we have more boards left to recover the deficit. Not that there is much difference in the way we play the game whether we are ahead or behind. However, when you are down, it is more important to win the next set and to get some momentum going your way.

I spend a most enjoyable hour or so watching the highlights of yesterday's golf on ESPN. Of course, I'd rather be playing myself, but watching is the next best thing.

When I wander down towards the playing rooms, I spot Eric. Actually, I hear him long before I see him — he has found an empty ballroom with a piano and he is playing away. We each have our own way to relax and clear the cobwebs out of the brain.

One thing neither of us enjoy is watching our teammates on Vugraph. I find it much tougher than playing. However, we both believe strongly in team spirit, so we join forces and head towards the scoring area in plenty of time to ensure that we are there for the comparison at the end of the set

The word filtering out from the Vugraph Theater is that neither side is gaining much of an advantage. This assessment proves to be accurate — when we meet to score, the match is tied at 27-27. In the other semifinal, Canada leads Poland by 6 IMPs.

We go into the Open Room on Vugraph to play against Levy-Mari. We have played a great deal against Alain Levy, but mainly when he was playing with Mouiel. Although this pairing is fairly new, both Levy and Mari are very experienced, and fine players.

On the very first deal, with the opponents only vulnerable, Eric deals and we pick up:

♠ 10 3　♡ 10 5　♢ K J 5 2　♣ 10 9 8 5 2

Eric opens with a limited (11-15 HCP) **one heart** and Levy, on our right, passes. **Would you pass?**

I don't psyche much but it's hard to resist it here. There is a very good chance that the opponents have a vulnerable game, and bidding **one spade** will make it tougher for them, particularly if spades is their fit.

Mari overcalls with a natural **one notrump** and Eric makes a Support **double**, showing a three-card spade raise. That's good news — we've bid and supported spades, which is the opponents' eight-card fit. It'll be tough for them to reach a spade contract now.

East passes and we remove ourselves to **two clubs**. LHO passes and Eric ups the ante to **three clubs**. Levy gives this some thought, but passes, as does everyone else.

WEST	NORTH	EAST	SOUTH
Mari	*Eric*	*Levy*	*Us*
	1♡	pass	1♠
1NT	dbl[1]	pass	2♣
pass	3♣	all pass	

1.　Three-card spade support.

West leads the queen of clubs and Eric puts down:

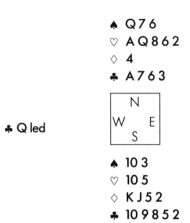

```
           ♠ Q76
           ♡ AQ862
           ◇ 4
           ♣ A763
              ┌─────┐
              │  N  │
♣ Q led    W  │     │  E
              │  S  │
              └─────┘
           ♠ 103
           ♡ 105
           ◇ KJ52
           ♣ 109852
```

We couldn't have hoped for a better auction after the One Spade bid. Playing in three non-vulnerable clubs gives us good odds to win a swing — we can only lose small, and we might gain a lot. Of course, that doesn't mean that we're looking to get out for a small minus — I always look for a way to make my contract!

Having taken the ace of clubs, **how should we continue?**

West is marked with most of the defensive strength, and he may easily have either the ♡K and/or the two top spades, so breaking a major doesn't look right. For want of anything better to do, we play dummy's diamond next.

Our jack loses to the queen and Mari plays the jack of clubs to his partner's king. A second diamond comes though, and we have to ruff in dummy.

Alain Levy

We have little choice but to play a spade now — the trick goes six, eight, ten, jack — and LHO returns a second spade to his partner's ace. When Levy now plays a third spade, we are in with a chance. We ruff in hand, finesse the heart queen, which wins, and cash the ace of hearts. A ruff sets up dummy's remaining hearts (the suit breaks 3-3), and there is still a trump in dummy to get there.

So it turns out that Levy could have beaten us by removing dummy's trump entry with a third round of diamonds instead of playing another spade. Had we played a spade instead of the diamond at Trick 2, though, he would not have had the chance to make that play.

Bridge is a game of guesses and mistakes. In retrospect, I think playing the diamond at Trick 2 was wrong. It's important to realize that everyone makes errors at the bridge table; the key is to make fewer than your opponents. When you do err, mental toughness is essential if you are going to be successful. You must maintain your composure and your best game on the next deal. Teammates make mistakes too and they will not have a problem if you come back to compare with a poor result. If you are in the habit of producing disastrous sets because that first error affects your performance on subsequent deals, though, you are likely to need to find new teammates with some regularity.

The ability to concentrate totally is part of the expert's arsenal. Being in sync as a partnership is a different kind of thing, and one that really only comes from total familiarity with each other's style and with the system that you are playing. And you can trust me when I tell you that even the most practiced partnerships have days when it would be easy to believe they had never met before, let alone played bridge together. Concentration, particularly in the card play, though, is primarily an individual thing. It's up to you to make sure that you are properly focused.

As we discover later, scoring plus 110 or minus 50 would have made a difference of only one IMP. Teammates win the board by bringing home 3NT when the defenders do not find the club lead. That's a 12-IMP pick-up on the first board of the set.

The early deals contain plenty of potential swings in both directions. Midway through the set, with just our side vulnerable, we deal and pick up:

$$\spadesuit \ A\,10\,9\,5 \quad \heartsuit \ K\,Q\,8\,7\,3\,2 \quad \diamondsuit \ 7 \quad \clubsuit \ A\,9$$

Opening **one heart** is clear. Christian Mari, on our left, enters with a **two clubs** overcall, and Eric makes a negative **double**. After a pass from Alain Levy, how many spades should we bid?

The answer playing with your regular partner will depend to some extent on your methods. In our system, Eric has a non-forcing Two Diamonds bid available. He cannot therefore have some 3-2-5-3 shape on which he is stuck for a bid, so this double pretty much guarantees four spades.

My gut feeling is that Three Spades is probably the 'right' bid, especially if there is any chance that responder does not hold four spades. Our decision to jump all the way to **four spades** is certainly very aggressive. Game might well not make, of course. However, there are lots of minimum hands on which partner will pass if you bid only Three Spades, where game will have excellent play.

> Whenever I have a choice between a slight underbid and a slight overbid, you have probably realized by now that I nearly always take the latter option. The reason for this is that the upside is usually greater if you are right.

The auction has been brief:

WEST	NORTH	EAST	SOUTH
Mari	Eric	Levy	Us
			1♡
2♣	dbl	pass	4♠
all pass			

West leads the king of clubs and Eric's meager collection does little to instill hope:

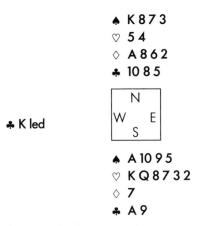

♠ K 8 7 3
♡ 5 4
◇ A 8 6 2
♣ 10 8 5

♣ K led

♠ A 10 9 5
♡ K Q 8 7 3 2
◇ 7
♣ A 9

On further inspection, it's clear that while we'll certainly need some luck, this contract is far from hopeless. However, there is a danger of losing control.

Generally, when trump control is an issue, it's better to do your side-suit work first. Drawing two rounds of trumps immediately will be a disaster if they don't break. Of course, we probably cannot make the contract if trumps divide 4-1, but neither do we want to go down three or four tricks vulnerable. Meanwhile, even if trumps split 3-2, we cannot afford to let the defenders draw a third round when they get in with the ace of hearts.

So we decide to set about the heart suit before getting involved with trumps. In a perfect world, we would prefer to lead twice towards the king-queen of hearts, but entries to dummy are limited. Besides, we think LHO has the ace of hearts anyway.

So, we lead the heart king at Trick 2… and RHO captures the trick with his ace — not the best of starts! Levy plays a club, which Mari wins with the jack. A switch to the king of diamonds comes next.

We take this with dummy's ace of diamonds and play a heart to the queen. When West ruffs and forces us with another high club as East pitches a diamond, things do not look great.

After ruffing the third round of clubs, we lead a heart and ruff in dummy. The king of spades and a spade to the ace draw the remaining trumps, which now divide 2-1, and a further heart ruff sets up our long cards in the suit. We still have a trump left with which to re-enter our hand — six trump tricks, two hearts and two aces comes to ten. Hmmm — how would you have rated our chances if you had been told that we would not score a trick with either the king or queen of hearts?

I learn later that the same contract was also made on an identical line of play at one table in the other semifinal too, which means that two world-class East players missed their chance. Notice what happens if East ruffs the third round of clubs with the queen of spades: we can overruff with the ace, but we cannot then pick up West's spade jack, ruff two hearts in dummy, and still get back to hand to enjoy the long heart winners.

Christian Mari

At the other table in our match, the French South rebid only Two Spades after an identical start to the auction. He also made only eight tricks, so we pick up 11 IMPs on the deal.

The remainder of the set does not go so well, though. The two double-figure swings that we have seen here are our only major gains in the stanza and they are more than offset by some large swings in the minus column. We lose a high-scoring set by 24 IMPs, 31-55. It's still early days, though.

In the other semifinal, Canada leads Poland by fourteen.

Eric and I remain North-South in the Open Room for the final set of the day, this time against Paul Chemla and Michel Perron. Paul is probably the most famous French player of all time and he is one of the truly great card players of our day. Eric does a great impression of Chemla, but Paul has an excellent sense of humor and he would find it amusing. Perron is a much quieter personality, but he too is a great player. He beat us single-handedly in the 1992 Olympiad final, and in so doing earned the nickname of 'The Terminator'.

The segment starts with two dull game hands. Then, with our side only vulnerable, RHO deals and we pick up:

♠ K 2   ♡ 8 7 5 3   ◇ 7   ♣ Q J 10 8 7 6

Chemla, on our right, opens **one heart**. We pass and, after a **one spade** response from Perron, Eric comes in with a natural **one notrump** overcall. After a pass on our right, **how should we proceed?**

Our choices are to get out to a club partscore, to invite game with a jump in clubs, or to raise directly to the notrump game.

Paul Chemla

Bridge is a partnership game, and experience has taught me that consulting partner is usually a good idea on a hand like this. Turning a plus score into a minus is bad news and it is therefore important not to overbid too much when the hand belongs to your side. It's on those hands where you are supposed to get a fairly large minus score anyway that you should be prepared to risk conceding a larger minus in exchange for the chance to go plus.

You can also afford to be very aggressive when you don't think partner will be able to know what the right hand is, but that is not the case here. There is also quite a difference between this auction and one where partner has opened One Notrump. Once partner opens one notrump (whatever range that shows in your methods), his shape and strength are fairly narrowly defined. In competitive auctions, there is always a greater variance of hands, in terms both of high card points and also of distribution. After all, they may be bidding his suits, and then he has only two choices — pass and One Notrump. Sometimes he will simply have too much to pass.

Because partner's range is very wide, he is more likely to know what to do if we consult him. We therefore elect to make an invitational jump to Three Clubs, and Eric passes quickly.

WEST	NORTH	EAST	SOUTH
Perron	Eric	Chemla	Us
		1♡	pass
1♠	1NT	pass	3♣
all pass			

West leads the heart queen and, when Eric puts down the dummy, it is easy to see why he did not feel up to accepting our invitation:

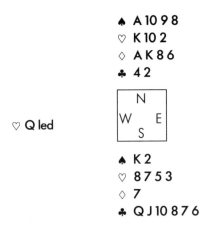

♠ A 10 9 8
♡ K 10 2
◇ A K 8 6
♣ 4 2

♡ Q led

♠ K 2
♡ 8 7 5 3
◇ 7
♣ Q J 10 8 7 6

West's heart queen is clearly a singleton, so things do not look good. If we cover with dummy's king, the defenders will quickly take two hearts and a heart ruff, with the two top trumps still to come later. We therefore play low from dummy.

East follows with the six of hearts and we contribute the seven, trying to make the six look high to encourage a spade shift. After some thought, Perron indeed switches to a low spade. Chemla does not cover dummy's eight but it would make no difference if he did.

We unblock the spade king, return to dummy in diamonds, and cash our two pointed-suit winners to discard hearts. When we then lead a club from dummy, Chemla rises with the ace, cashes the ace of hearts, and plays another heart through. All that remains is to guess the trump position. **How would you play?**

West has shown up with five hearts and three spades so far. If diamonds are 4-4, then his ace of clubs was singleton and there's nothing we can do. A 5-3 diamond split feels more likely than 6-2, so we should play East for a 3-5-3-2 shape. Are his clubs ace-king or ace-nine? My gut feeling is the former — he might have played low on the first round with ♣A-9, for example.

Having decided to play East for ace-king doubleton in trumps, it is a simple matter to ruff the heart high and exit with a low trump. East wins perforce with the king and plays another heart, but we again ruff high and lay down our other high club to draw West's nine.

This is the full deal:

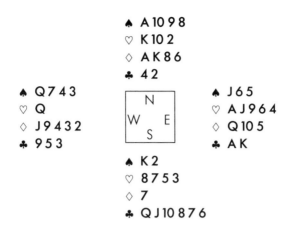

```
                    ♠ A 10 9 8
                    ♡ K 10 2
                    ◇ A K 8 6
                    ♣ 4 2
  ♠ Q 7 4 3           N          ♠ J 6 5
  ♡ Q                            ♡ A J 9 6 4
  ◇ J 9 4 3 2     W     E        ◇ Q 10 5
  ♣ 9 5 3           S            ♣ A K
                    ♠ K 2
                    ♡ 8 7 5 3
                    ◇ 7
                    ♣ Q J 10 8 7 6
```

Our plus 110 turns out to be a useful result. At the other table, the French North-South pair came to rest in Two Hearts after our East had opened with a strong notrump. Declarer could have scrambled seven tricks by taking two ruffs in the South hand, but he tried to make the contract by setting up the clubs. He could not then handle the 5-1 trump break and ended up three down. Plus 300 for our East-West pair means a 9-IMP swing on what looked like a nothing deal.

> It's very important to go plus on these 'small deals'. Turning a minus into a small plus is probably worth about 4 IMPs on average, and those little swings can add up really quickly into a significant number.

We get the better of a couple more partscore hands, and then comes something that looks even more promising. With neither side vulnerable, we deal and pick up:

♠ A Q 10 5 ♡ 10 7 ◇ A K Q 8 5 ♣ A Q

This hand is clearly worth a strong, artificial **one club** in anyone's book. LHO passes and Eric responds with a game-forcing **one heart**, showing either a positive (8+ HCP) with five or more spades, or a balanced 11-13. We bid a natural **two diamonds** and Eric jumps to **three hearts**, showing at least 5-5 in the majors. There is no decision to make yet — as Eric's hand is still unlimited, we simply set the trump suit by bidding **three spades**.

Eric's options now include bidding Three Notrump with good slam values or cuebidding as a mild slam try. His decision to make a simple raise to **four spades** is therefore his weakest available action.

Our style is to show any first- or second-round control in a cuebidding auction but we do not cuebid shortage controls in partner's long suit, so we can infer that Eric has short diamonds. He would certainly have cuebid in hearts with both the ace and king, but he could have the spade king and one top heart as this is not an obligatory cuebid situation. Even if his hearts are only king high, slam will only fail if the ace is offside and they lead the suit — good odds. Besides, I think they rate to lead a club on this auction, so I don't need much at all from Eric.

Eric Rodwell

We therefore press on with **four notrump** and Eric's **five diamonds** response confirms one key card. It's decision time!

Our general philosophy as far as slams go is, of course, to bid the ones that make and to stay out of those that don't. Like most good pairs, we want a small slam to be better than 50% and a grand slam significantly more than that. Seven down one is a killer result.

We think this one rates to be 50% or better, particularly as we expect a club lead — **six spades**.

WEST	NORTH	EAST	SOUTH
Perron	*Eric*	*Chemla*	*Us*
			1♣[1]
pass	1♡[2]	pass	2◇
pass	3♡[3]	pass	3♠
pass	4♠	pass	4NT[4]
pass	5◇[5]	pass	6♠
all pass			

1. Strong, artificial.
2. Game-forcing, either 11-13 balanced or 8+ with five or more spades.
3. At least 5-5 in the majors.
4. RKCB.
5. One key card.

When dummy appears, the most glaring absence is the expected heart control. However, Perron's opening lead is not a heart, but the two of clubs.

This is the full hand:

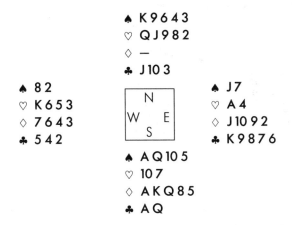

```
              ♠ K 9 6 4 3
              ♡ Q J 9 8 2
              ◇ —
              ♣ J 10 3
  ♠ 8 2                      ♠ J 7
  ♡ K 6 5 3        N         ♡ A 4
  ◇ 7 6 4 3    W     E       ◇ J 10 9 2
  ♣ 5 4 2          S         ♣ K 9 8 7 6
              ♠ A Q 10 5
              ♡ 10 7
              ◇ A K Q 8 5
              ♣ A Q
```

When we play the jack of clubs from dummy at Trick 1, it is virtually impossible for East to withhold his king. With the ten of clubs established for a heart discard, the contract is guaranteed against anything but a 4-0 trump break. As it happens, with

diamonds breaking 4-4, the club play is irrelevant. Plus 980 and surely another double-figure swing to the good guys...

Alas not; the French at the other table also blast into the slam from the South seat and our West also leads a club. We had to bid this one to avoid a loss on the board!

Towards the end of the set, with only the opponents vulnerable, we deal and pick up:

♠ J 9 7 5 4 2   ♡ 7 3   ◊ A Q 8   ♣ A Q

We open **one spade** and, after a pass from Perron, Eric raises to **two spades**.

> There are players who automatically blast into game whenever their partner voluntarily raises their six-card suit, but this policy only seems to work consistently for you if you're from Pakistan. My view is that this hand is worth only a game try. If partner refuses, how good a contract is game likely to be?

Things change, however, when Chemla comes in with a **three diamonds** overcall. This improves our hand appreciably — our diamonds are effectively now ace-king and, as RHO's suit is poor, he must have a decent hand to come in at unfavorable vulnerability. Thus the club finesse is more likely to work too.

It is not even a close decision now — we have a clear **four spades** bid. The auction has been a simple one:

WEST	NORTH	EAST	SOUTH
Perron	Eric	Chemla	Us
			1♠
pass	2♠	3♦	4♠
all pass			

Perron leads the two of diamonds and Eric produces:

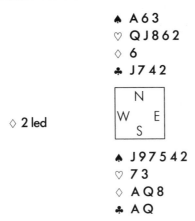

♠ A 6 3
♡ Q J 8 6 2
♦ 6
♣ J 7 4 2

◊ 2 led

♠ J 9 7 5 4 2
♡ 7 3
♦ A Q 8
♣ A Q

We seem to have two hearts and a trump to lose, so the club finesse will have to be right. **Can anything be done if we have two trump losers?**

Perhaps — if we can dispose of one of the hearts. Doing so might be possible if we can set up the jack of clubs, and that's actually not unlikely. Since East has long diamonds he is therefore odds-on to have the shorter club holding. Let's see what happens.

We capture the diamond jack with the queen at Trick 1 and immediately ruff a diamond in dummy. The club finesse wins and we unblock the ace of clubs. We then play a trump to dummy's ace, both defenders following with low cards. East's king pops up on the third round of clubs and we ruff it away.

We're almost home now — we ruff the ace of diamonds in dummy and lead the established jack of clubs, pitching a heart. The defenders can score two trump tricks and one heart only and it matters not whether the trumps were originally 2-2 or 3-1.

This is the full hand:

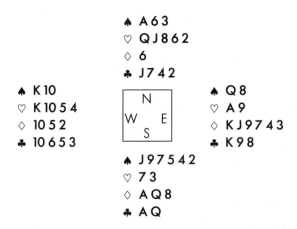

As it happens, trumps were 2-2 anyway, so just about any line of play will produce ten tricks after the diamond lead. However, the contract could have been beaten — the defenders must start with three rounds of hearts. East ruffs with the spade queen and West's ♠K-10 represents the setting trick.

Our teammates' defense was not tested, since the French South bid only Three Spades at his second turn after the same start to the auction. Our West competed to Four Diamonds, which bought the contract, thankfully undoubled. Declarer managed just eight tricks, but that was still only minus 200 — a 6-IMP swing on the board.

Momentum is a *huge* factor in long team matches. If you get it, you want to keep it. When the final deal of the set arrives, it is therefore something of a disappointment. The momentum is very much with us at the moment and we would be quite happy to play another sixteen deals without stopping. The French, by contrast, cannot wait to get away from the table to regroup. They will be delighted that this is the last set of the day.

Our hand on the final deal has considerable potential, though. With neither side vulnerable, LHO deals and we pick up:

♠ A   ♡ 10 6 3   ◇ 9 8   ♣ A K Q 10 9 4 2

Perron, on our left, opens **one diamond** and Eric comes in with a Michaels **two diamonds** overcall, showing at least 5-5 in the majors. **What are your thoughts?**

Sure, we might be cold for a slam in clubs — why shouldn't partner hold something like:

♠ K x x x x   ♡ A K x x x   ◇ x   ♣ x x

Opposite that hand, Six Clubs is a pretty good spot. The problem is that we have no way to find out if he has the right hand for slam. When the opponents open the bidding, you are automatically defensive bidders. On the vast majority of deals, you need to be able to compete effectively. To do so, you must give up the tools that enable you investigate the odd, rare slam.

The one thing we do know here is that we have an eight-card major-suit fit. Looking further than game is asking for trouble, so we jump to **four hearts**. (Besides, it's possible that burying the club suit may prove advantageous in the play.) The auction has been brief:

WEST	NORTH	EAST	SOUTH
Perron	*Eric*	*Chemla*	*Us*
1◇	2◇	pass	4♡
all pass			

West leads the ◇A and Eric puts down a fairly moderate dummy:

♠ K J 7 6 4
♡ Q 9 8 7 4
◇ K J
♣ 8

◇ A led

```
      N
  W       E
      S
```

♠ A
♡ 10 6 3
◇ 9 8
♣ A K Q 10 9 4 2

Perron continues with a second diamond to dummy's king at Trick 2. **What are you thinking?**

Our gut feeling says that West has probably led from a diamond suit headed by the ace-queen, which means that he is only looking for one more defensive trick — i.e. he has both top hearts.

We do not have either the entries or the trump length or solidity to try ruffing out the spades, so we'll need to score club tricks. First, though, we'll have to draw some trumps. So, we cross to the ♠A and play a heart on which Perron plays low smoothly.

The contract has no chance if West's hearts are A-K-J-x, so we rise with the queen of hearts, felling East's jack. **What now?**

Playing another trump is no good — West will win, cash his second trump winner, and exit with a club. He will then be able to ruff the third or fourth round of clubs, leaving us with a spade loser.

Now is the time to play clubs. When both defenders follow to the first two rounds, we are home. West has no answer to the third club winner. If he discards a spade, so will dummy and we cannot then be prevented from scoring either a spade ruff in hand or the rest of the club suit. If he ruffs low, we will overruff, ruff a spade in hand, and lead another club winner. Either way, West can score only his high trumps.

In fact, on the third round of clubs Perron ruffs in with the king of hearts. He continues with ace and another heart, so we win in hand with the ten and claim, using the clubs; plus 420.

At the other table, the French North overcalled One Spade at his first turn and South ended up playing in a club partial. Ten tricks were made. Minus 130, and another 7 IMPs in the plus column.

Eric and I know that we have a good card. Just how good is not apparent until we began scoring up. Apart from letting through the slam with two cashing hearts against it, which was a flat board, teammates are also very good and we win the set 54-1. We therefore lead by 29 IMPs at the midway point of the match.

Meanwhile, the Canadians win their third consecutive stanza and have extended their lead in the other semifinal to 38 IMPs.

For the first set of the second day, Eric and I go into the Closed Room as East-West. Our opponents will be Franck Multon and Herve Mouiel.

Multon is young and subject to becoming emotional, but Mouiel is very steady and should be an ideal partner for him. We have played against Herve many times, most often when he was playing with Levy — we played the Burgay Notrump Challenge Match against them, for example. It was with Multon, though, that Mouiel was playing when they beat us in the 1997 Bermuda Bowl final in Africa.

A few deals into the set, with only our side vulnerable, Eric deals and we pick up:

♠ A Q 10 9 7 6 3   ♡ K 3   ◇ K 2   ♣ 7 5

Eric opens proceedings with a strong, artificial **one club** and Multon, on our right, comes in with a **three diamonds** overcall. We have no problem yet — **three spades** is natural and forcing, so that seems obvious. Mouiel raises to **five diamonds** and Eric passes.

We have reversed the meaning of pass and double in these high-level competitive situations. Thus, a double would suggest a spade fit and a suitable offensive hand, whereas a pass is usually regressive, asking me to double — a strong suggestion that we should defend. If he then pulls the double, that shows a strong slam try. (The method works well in clearly forcing auctions.)

This spade suit does not need much in the way of support. Also, the vulnerability suggest playing rather than defending. But if partner is voting to defend, it is fairly clear to agree with his assessment when we are looking at king doubleton in the opponents' suit.

We duly **double**, which ends the auction:

WEST	NORTH	EAST	SOUTH
Us	Mouiel	Eric	Multon
		1♣[1]	3◊
3♠	5◊	pass[2]	pass
dbl	all pass		

1. Strong, artificial.
2. Forcing and suggesting defending.

Although there is an inference that Eric is short in spades, leading the ace can be wrong in too many ways. Neither does a red-suit attack look particularly attractive, so we settle on a club by default. This is what we can see:

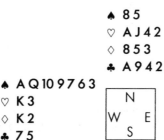

```
                    ♠ 8 5
                    ♡ A J 4 2
                    ◊ 8 5 3
                    ♣ A 9 4 2
    ♠ A Q 10 9 7 6 3   ┌─────────┐
    ♡ K 3              │   N     │
    ◊ K 2            W │       E │
    ♣ 7 5              │   S     │
                       └─────────┘
```

Declarer wins the first trick with the ace of clubs, crosses to the ace of hearts, and plays a diamond to his queen and our king.
Now what?

Declarer's play in the heart suit is interesting. If we don't cash the king now, though, there is a danger that we will be thrown in with it later to lead a spade.

Herve Mouiel

We revert to clubs after cashing the king of hearts but declarer has the tempo he needs now — hearts is his second suit. He ruffs the second round of clubs, forces out Eric's ace of diamonds, and eventually scores four heart tricks, three trumps and the ace of clubs — only three down; plus 500.

Had we forced declarer rather than cashing the heart king, he would have been unable to draw Eric's third trump and we would have scored a sixth trick.

Fortunately, the difference between plus 500 and plus 800 proves to be just 2 IMPs. At the other table (and at both tables in the other semifinal), East opened Eric's hand with a strong notrump and the players with our hand drove on to Five Spades. The defenders found their club ruff to beat this contract at all three tables, so our 500 actually looks pretty good; plus 11 IMPs.

If I am playing right at the top of my game, I don't expect to make any clear errors. But there are many situations in which one cannot deduce the winning play for sure. No one can get all of these right. You just hope to 'guess' right fairly often. Sometimes your incorrect guess is still better than theirs, so you gain IMPs anyway.

The next few boards are rather dull. We concede a couple of soft partscore results, but there is little potential for either side to make significant gains. Then, on the penultimate deal of the set, RHO deals with both sides vulnerable and we pick up:

♠ Q 8   ♡ A K Q 8 2   ◊ 9 6 5 2   ♣ J 6

Multon opens **one club** on our right and we have an easy **one heart** overcall. **One spade** from Mouiel is followed by Eric's raise to **two hearts** and two passes. Mouiel backs in with a takeout **double**, which Multon removes to **two notrump**. Mouiel's raise to **three notrump** ends the auction and leaves us on lead.

WEST	NORTH	EAST	SOUTH
Us	Mouiel	Eric	Multon
			1♣
1♡	1♠	2♡	pass
pass	dbl	pass	2NT
pass	3NT	all pass	

We lead the queen of hearts and dummy comes down with:

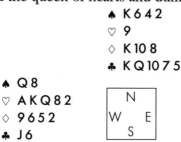

♠ K 6 4 2
♡ 9
◇ K 10 8
♣ K Q 10 7 5

♠ Q 8
♡ A K Q 8 2
◇ 9 6 5 2
♣ J 6

Eric follows with the seven of hearts (upside-down attitude for the jack) and declarer with the five.

How should we continue?

Eric will almost certainly have only three hearts for his single raise and his seven denies the jack, so declarer has ♡J-10-x-x or ♡J-x-x-x. Either way, there is clearly no future in continuing hearts from our side.

If Eric started with ♡10-7-x and an ace, we can beat the contract by putting him in for a lead through declarer's heart jack. Must we commit ourselves to either a spade or a diamond switch, though?

With 4-4 in the minors, the French style is to open One Diamond rather than One Club, so declarer can have only eight top tricks, no matter which two aces he holds. It looks right to exit passively with a club and hope that we will know what to do by the time we get another chance.

Declarer wins the ace of clubs and cashes five tricks in the suit. Eric's first discard is the three of spades (encouraging), then the four of hearts, clarifying the position in that suit (he does not have the ten), and finally a diamond (showing an odd number — obviously three). This makes things easy for us — we can safely throw our two low hearts and a diamond.

Declarer cashes three diamond winners and exits with a heart. Declarer threw a spade on the fifth round of clubs, so he has only a singleton left in the suit. It is therefore safe for us to cash our third heart winner and play the queen of spades. Eric takes the last two tricks with the ace-jack of spades — one down; plus 100. This is the full hand:

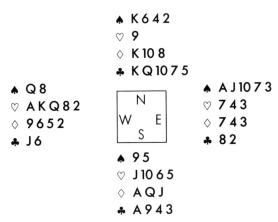

We could have both hastened the play and beaten the contract by at least two by switching to the queen of spades at Trick 2, but that could just as easily have let the game come home on a different layout.

At the other table, our South opened One Heart playing four-card majors and subsequently denied a fifth heart en route to the same Three Notrump contract. Perron, sitting West for the French, put his eggs all in one basket by leading a low heart at Trick 1. Reasonable though this plan might have been, he ran into the worst possible scenario, giving declarer his ninth trick on the lead. On any other opening, the defenders at least get a second chance.

We pick up a useful 12 IMPs on this deal to go with the eleven we gained on the other deal early in the stanza, but little else goes our way in a relatively dull set of boards. Still, we win the set by 3 IMPs (25-22), extending our lead to 32 IMPs with two 16-board sets left to play.

The set is also tight in the other match, but Canada gains another 7 IMPs and now lead by forty-five.

We are back in the Closed Room for the fifth set, this time against Mari and Levy. On the second board, vulnerable against not, we deal and pick up:

♠ K 10 5 2 ♡ A K 8 7 ◇ Q J 9 7 ♣ K

Many Strong Club pairs would not consider this hand good enough for a **one club** opening, but we are well-known for testing the lower limits of our system's strong bid rather more often than most. This is not a good 16-count, but there is too much of a risk of missing game if we do not open One Club.

Christian Mari, on our left, joins in with a natural **two clubs** overcall and Eric responds **two spades** — positive values, five or more spades, and forcing to game. Levy dramatically increases the preempt with a leap to **five clubs** and we are in the hot seat.

We have already discussed some of the reasons behind switching Pass and Double in these forcing situations. Here, our options are: to bid Five Spades, which would not be invitational; to double, showing a spade fit and a hand that is unsure what to do, or; to pass, asking Eric to double. Passing now and then pulling Eric's likely double would show serious slam interest — something we clearly do not have, having already opened a Strong Club. If we pass, we will therefore have to sit for Eric's double. The real question is whether to bid Five Spades or just to suggest we bid on with a double.

Since bidding on is not clear, a **double** which shows both the spade fit and uncertainty seems to describe our hand perfectly — this method is designed precisely for this type of situation.

Our double ends a brief but explosive auction:

WEST	NORTH	EAST	SOUTH
Eric	Levy	Us	Mari
		1♣[1]	2♣
2♠	5♣	dbl[2]	all pass

1. Strong, artificial.
2. Equivalent to a forcing pass.

Eric leads the three of spades (third and fifth) and Levy puts down a dummy filled with good news for our side:

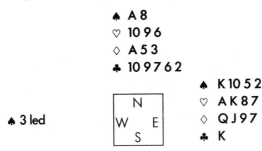

Declarer ducks at Trick 1 and we win with the king of spades.

How should we proceed?

The odds favor South holding the missing high trumps and it also looks like declarer has the spade queen. Eric must therefore have the missing red-suit honors to make up his positive response. Switching to diamonds now will ensure that we untangle the suit if declarer happens to have started with ◊ 10-x-x-x.

The diamond seven is covered by the eight, king and ace. After playing a trump to the king, ace and jack, declarer concedes four red-suit tricks; three down. Plus 500.

This is the full deal:

```
                    ♠ A 8
                    ♡ 10 9 6
                    ◇ A 5 3
                    ♣ 10 9 7 6 2
♠ J 9 7 4 3                          ♠ K 10 5 2
♡ Q J 4 3         ┌─────────┐        ♡ A K 8 7
◇ K 6 4          │    N    │        ◇ Q J 9 7
♣ J            W │         │ E      ♣ K
                 │    S    │
                 └─────────┘
                    ♠ Q 6
                    ♡ 5 2
                    ◇ 10 8 2
                    ♣ A Q 8 5 4 3
```

As the cards lie, it matters little how we defend after the initial spade lead. The deal has been won in the bidding. So often, a Strong Club opening acts like a red rag to a bull to the opponents, particularly when they are at favorable vulnerability. Of course, that sometimes works to their advantage, but you would be surprised at how often they simply give away a penalty when we can make little or nothing.

I have my own ideas on the best way to defend against a Strong Club opening (a Three Spades overcall is usually the most effective defense!). However, there are some secrets I'm just not willing to share — we play a Strong Club system and I don't want to make my life even more difficult.

Christian Mari

At the other table, the French East opened One Diamond and our South did not have enough for a two-level overcall. East-West therefore bid to Four Spades uncontested. Declarer won the opening heart lead in his hand and made the normal play of running the nine of spades to South's queen; one down. Plus 100 looks like a fairly normal result to our teammates, and they are delighted to gain twelve unexpected IMPs.

Towards the end of the set, with only our side vulnerable, LHO deals and we pick up this promising collection:

♠ Q ♡ A J 8 7 ◇ K 8 3 ♣ K Q 10 8 2

As dealer, Christian Mari opens Four Spades, which is followed by two passes. **Would you take any action?**

Our methods over four-level major-suit openings are the same whether we are in second or fourth seat. We play a double of a Four Hearts to say, 'feel free to bid Four Spades.' A double of Four Spades, though, will usually be passed, but partner can bid 4NT with a decent two-suited hand that expects to make at the five-level if a fit is found.

Our offense-defense ratio here is very low, and venturing to the five-level on our own is not an option. We do not like to pass decent hands in this position, though, so we elect to **double**, ending a brief auction.

WEST	NORTH	EAST	SOUTH
Eric	Levy	Us	Mari
			4♠
pass	pass	dbl	all pass

Eric leads the five of hearts (third and fifth) and Levy produces about an average dummy:

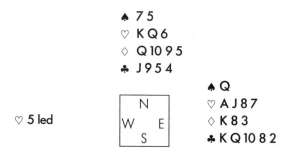

♡ 5 led

Declarer calls for the king of hearts from dummy.
How do you defend?

We can tell from the heart spot led that declarer has at least
two hearts, so there is no hurry to take our ace. We therefore
allow the king of hearts to hold Trick 1.

Declarer plays a trump to our queen and his king, which
wins, and then plays the jack of spades, which Eric captures with
the ace. We win the second round of hearts, cash our second
winner in the suit, and deliver partner's ruff. We have a trick in
each minor still to come; three down. Plus 500.

This is the full deal:

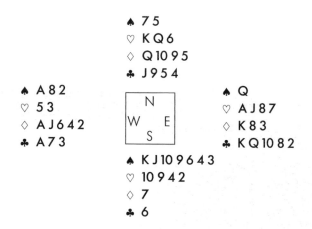

With both heart honors onside, and thus no entry to South's
spades, we could have made ten tricks in notrump. Getting there
after a Four Spades opening is just too tough, though.

Alas, at the other table, our South decided that his hand was worth only Three Spades. The French East had a routine balancing seat takeout double and West an equally clear Three Notrump bid. Declarer managed ten tricks and thus we needed to collect the maximum from Four Spades Doubled just to hold the loss on the deal to 4 IMPs.

This proves to be another close, low-scoring set of boards. We gain a further 3 IMPs on the stanza (20-17), increasing our lead to 35 IMPs with sixteen boards remaining. It's a significant difference, but by no means an insurmountable one for a team as good as the French, particularly if the cards should turn wild again.

In the other semifinal, the Canadians look to be safely through to the final — they now lead by eighty-one. If we can hold on, it will be an all-ACBL Bermuda Bowl final for only the second time in history.

Alain Levy

It is our choice of opponents for the final set and we elect to return to the Open Room against Chemla-Perron. We start with two flat game hands, and then comes something with a little more potential. With only the opponents vulnerable, we deal and pick up:

♠ J 10 9 6 2   ♡ K 10 8 4 2   ◇ 10 3   ♣ 7

If we were playing 'big catch-up', I might consider an off-center opening bid, a weak two in one of the majors perhaps, but not in any other situation. In general, we try to play the same style of bridge pretty much regardless of the score. One thing is certain — you cannot sit on a lead by being cautious. That's the worst thing one can do. You should just continue playing in the same style that has earned you the lead in the first place. If your natural style is to be very aggressive, then you should continue to play that way.

Following our pass, Perron opens **one club**. Eric overcalls **one diamond** and Chemla responds **one heart**. **Would you pass now or bid your spades?**

We are at favorable vulnerability and it is quite possible that we need to be saving if partner has four spades. You will never find your spade fit if you pass now, and introducing the spades is cheap. Partner will not expect the World's Fair — he'll remember that you did not open with a weak two-bid in spades.

We therefore join in with **one spade** and Perron jumps to **two notrump** — strong and natural. Eric bids **three hearts** next, which we play as showing a good raise with four-card spade support.

Chemla bids game — **three notrump**, and we have a decision to make. **Should we save or let them play?**

Favorable vulnerability is a powerful weapon when you have a good fit and this hand is a classic example. I think it's clear to bid, so we press on to **four spades**. Perron passes, inviting his partner to bid again but, after some consideration, Chemla closes proceedings with a **double**.

WEST	NORTH	EAST	SOUTH
Perron	*Eric*	*Chemla*	*Us*
			pass
1♣	1◇	1♡	1♠
2NT	3♡[1]	3NT	4♠
pass	pass	dbl	all pass

1.   Good spade raise with four-card support.

West leads the king of clubs and Eric puts down:

```
              ♠ Q 8 4 3
              ♡ A
              ◇ K 7 5 4 2
              ♣ 10 6 4
                 ┌─────────┐
                 │    N    │
  ♣ K led        │ W     E │
                 │    S    │
                 └─────────┘
              ♠ J 10 9 6 2
              ♡ K 10 8 4 2
              ◇ 10 3
              ♣ 7
```

West continues with a second high club at Trick 2. We ruff in hand and play a diamond, West rising with the ace and forcing us with a third round of clubs.

We cross to the king of diamonds and ruff a third round. When they break 3-3, we are left with the straightforward task of knocking out the defenders' trump honors. We lose just two trumps and two side-suit aces; one down — minus 100.

This is the full deal:

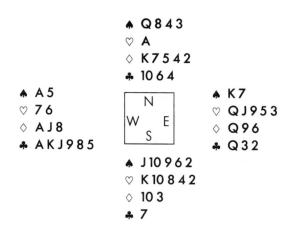

```
              ♠ Q 8 4 3
              ♡ A
              ◇ K 7 5 4 2
              ♣ 10 6 4
  ♠ A 5          ┌───────┐      ♠ K 7
  ♡ 7 6          │   N   │      ♡ Q J 9 5 3
  ◇ A J 8        │ W   E │      ◇ Q 9 6
  ♣ A K J 9 8 5  │   S   │      ♣ Q 3 2
                 └───────┘
              ♠ J 10 9 6 2
              ♡ K 10 8 4 2
              ◇ 10 3
              ♣ 7
```

Perron did as much as he could, and Chemla might have pressed on to the cold Four Notrump had he been sure that his partner held a sixth club. With such slow values, though, it was difficult for him to be sure there would be a tenth trick available quickly enough.

At the other table, our West opened a Strong Club and North passed. Over the One Diamond negative, the French South bid 1NT to show the majors. West bid a natural Two Clubs and North now jumped to Four Spades. There was then virtually no chance of East-West reaching Four Notrump, so doubling and collecting plus 100 was the best they could do, since the realistic alternative of bidding on to Five Clubs would have produced a minus score.

A hard-earned flat board all around!

Michel Perron

Little of note happens during this fairly quiet set but we seem to get the better of things. This, the penultimate board of the match, is typical of how the stanza has gone. With only our side vulnerable, we deal and pick up:

♠ 9 6 3   ♡ A K 10 8 7 6   ◇ K 10 2   ♣ 5

We open **one heart**. Eric responds **one spade** and we rebid **two hearts**, which is raised to game — **four hearts**.

Perron leads the queen of diamonds and, when dummy comes down, it looks very much like another dull flat game deal:

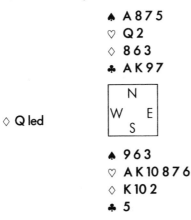

```
            ♠ A 8 7 5
            ♡ Q 2
            ◇ 8 6 3
            ♣ A K 9 7
                  N
◇ Q led      W       E
                  S
            ♠ 9 6 3
            ♡ A K 10 8 7 6
            ◇ K 10 2
            ♣ 5
```

East takes the opening lead with the ace of diamonds and returns the diamond nine. We win with the king and play a heart to the queen and a second trump back to the ace, but West discards a diamond on this trick. Our ten tricks seem to have been reduced to nine. But have they?

How would you continue?

We have four side-suit tricks and thus need to score six trumps. In fact, we have a virtually guaranteed route to ten tricks here. We cash the two top clubs and ruff the third round of the suit. A spade to the ace puts us back in dummy for another club ruff and, with eight tricks already in the bag, we can now simply exit with either a spade or a diamond. At Trick 12, the defenders will have to lead into our ♡K-10; plus 620.

Another flat board? Not at all. Take a look at the full deal:

```
                    ♠ A 8 7 5
                    ♡ Q 2
                    ◇ 8 6 3
                    ♣ A K 9 7
   ♠ Q J 10 2      ┌──────────┐   ♠ K 4
   ♡ 3             │    N     │   ♡ J 9 5 4
   ◇ Q J 7 5 4     │ W     E  │   ◇ A 9
   ♣ Q 4 3         │    S     │   ♣ J 10 8 6 2
                    └──────────┘
                    ♠ 9 6 3
                    ♡ A K 10 8 7 6
                    ◇ K 10 2
                    ♣ 5
```

At the other table, our West led a spade at Trick 1 against the same contract, thereby removing a crucial entry from dummy. Declarer won and played a diamond towards the king, and our East did very well by rising with the ace. (We will leave you to work out the variations if you are so inclined, but trust us that if East ducks this trick, declarer can reduce his trumps to reach the same ending that we achieved.) East cashed the king of spades and exited with a second diamond to declarer's king. The French declarer then played a heart to the queen and a second trump back to the ace, getting the bad news. He could pitch one of his losers on dummy's top clubs, but the timing was now wrong for the endplay since he could not reduce his trump length sufficiently — one down; plus 100 and 12 IMPs in.

The Forbidden City

When it comes time to score the last set, we are not worried. We are confident that we have done enough to protect a 35-IMP lead. However, teammates produce an enormous set and it turns out to be a rout. We win the final stanza by 57 IMPs (70-13) and the match by a margin (92 IMPs) that looks much more comfortable than it felt.

Meanwhile, the Canadians lose 20 IMPs on the last set but still run out comfortable winners, defeating Poland by 61 IMPs.

The final of the Bermuda Bowl will be USA versus Canada. The match will be played over 160 boards, divided into ten 16-board segments played over three days. Play starts early tomorrow morning but we will still enjoy a couple of beers tonight with our teammates, with our friends from Canada, and with those French and Polish players who wish to drown their disappointment.

The Forbidden City

The Final

The Canadians have played well throughout the two weeks and clearly deserve their place in the final. Some spectators were surprised to see the Canadians still alive at this point, but we weren't. They certainly have the ability, and the inclusion of a talented young player (Gitelman) has made them a very strong team.

All six Canadian players are familiar opponents from Nationals at home and I consider all of them friends. I've known them all well for many years. They are all class guys and the good news is that if we don't win then I'll be very happy that they did.

Eric Kokish is a theorist. He is recognized as one of the world's best coaches and in fact is currently our team coach. Perhaps the only strike against Eric is that he is notoriously difficult to play with, but that does not seem to have been a factor during this event. His partner, Joey Silver, is a player with plenty of imagination and tremendous natural talent.

Fred Gitelman is a young player with plenty of promise, while George Mittelman has been around at the top levels forever, or so it seems. Collectively dubbed 'The Men' by Silver, they will be no pushover.

Boris Baran and Mark Molson are very experienced competitors with a host of Canadian national titles to their credit. They are also the longest-standing partnership on the Canadian team and it is my opinion that we will need to 'neutralize' them to win this match.

We might not originally have expected to meet the Canadians at this stage, but they are playing exceptionally well. We are confident, as always, but we will not be taking them lightly.

The final is a match of 160 boards divided into ten segments — four today, four tomorrow and the last two sets on the final day of the championships.

We start off in the Closed Room against Mittelman-Gitelman. The match opens with a dull game hand. Then, with the opponents only vulnerable, Eric deals and we pick up:

♠ J7 ♡ A 10 6 5 3 ◇ 7 5 3 2 ♣ 6 3

Eric passes and RHO, Mittelman, opens **one club**.

Nothing good ever seems to happen when I pass in this type of situation. If left alone in the auction, good players tend to do very well. Almost certainly, the opponents can make game.

Making a bid that potentially shows strength seems to be the best tactic, so we enter with a **one heart** overcall.

Gitelman now cuebids **two hearts**, a game-forcing club raise (so much for talking them out of game) and Eric competes with a gentle raise to **three hearts**.

Eric had two ways to show a moderate heart fit — double or Three Hearts. His choice of Three Hearts is primarily designed to steal their space in what is not a constructive position, but by definition (we're at the three-level) also shows better playing strength than would a double.

Rightie bids out his shape with **three spades**, Gitelman continues with **four clubs**, and Mittelman raises himself to **five clubs**.

WEST	NORTH	EAST	SOUTH
Us	Gitelman	Eric	Mittelman
		pass	1♣
1♡	2♡	3♡	3♠
pass	4♣	pass	5♣
all pass			

We lead the ace of hearts and switch to a diamond. This is the full deal:

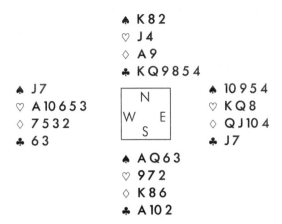

```
              ♠ K 8 2
              ♡ J 4
              ◇ A 9
              ♣ K Q 9 8 5 4
♠ J 7                          ♠ 10 9 5 4
♡ A 10 6 5 3    N              ♡ K Q 8
◇ 7 5 3 2    W   E             ◇ Q J 10 4
♣ 6 3           S             ♣ J 7
              ♠ A Q 6 3
              ♡ 9 7 2
              ◇ K 8 6
              ♣ A 10 2
```

Declarer wins the diamond switch, draws two rounds of trumps, and claims eleven or twelve tricks depending on the spade break. With spades 4-2 we concede eleven tricks; minus 600. Had declarer played the hand out, though, Eric would have been squeezed in the pointed suits for the twelfth trick.

Have you noticed why this is likely to be a poor result?

George Mittelman

Had we not overcalled, the opponents would probably have ended in Three Notrump. Our teammates do just that and the defenders cash the first five tricks for a 12-IMP loss.

Still, our aggressive style has been worth thousands for IMPs over the years and one has to accept some losses from it too. Indeed, I consider this type of loss to be normal playing luck.

A couple of deals later, with both sides vulnerable, we deal and pick up:

♠ 8 ♡ K 10 6 3 2 ◇ 2 ♣ Q J 9 6 5 4

I am all in favor of preempting, but doing so on two-suiters is very risky — it is much too likely that we belong in our second suit. It is certainly not impossible that opening Two Hearts or Three Clubs could land us in a silly contract with a game or even a slam cold in the other suit. Let's pass and see how things develop.

Gitelman starts things rolling with **one spade**. After a pass from Eric, Mittelman responds with a forcing **one notrump**. We have a bid to show a heart-club two-suiter —**three clubs**. Our convention card defines this as 'aggressive but not crazy'. Having already passed, we're 6-5 with all of our points in our suits — I'd say this hand fits the definition perfectly.

Gitelman **doubles** and Eric gives preference to **three hearts**.

I learn later that the Vugraph commentators were critical of our teammates' failure to double their opponents at the two-level, where they could have collected 500. I wonder whether Eric would have considered our Three Clubs overcall 'not crazy' if he had been left to declare Three Hearts Doubled!

Thankfully, though, opponents do not always stop to double when they should. Fred intends his double of Three Clubs as 'strong balanced' but George interprets it as 'strong, quasi-balanced with support for the unbid suit — diamonds'.

Mittelman therefore advances with **four diamonds** when a double would have been a better option from a Canadian perspective. Expecting a good diamond suit, Gitelman raises confidently to game — **five diamonds**. Eric's **double** is the final positive bid in an eventful auction.

WEST	NORTH	EAST	SOUTH
Us	*Gitelman*	*Eric*	*Mittelman*
pass	1♠	pass	1NT
3♣[1]	dbl	3♡	4◇
pass	5◇	dbl	all pass

1.   Clubs and hearts.

We lead our singleton spade and dummy comes down with:

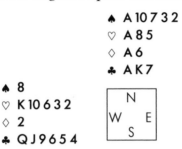

Declarer wins with the ace of spades and plays ace and another diamond. Eric puts in the jack and declarer wins with the king. Now comes the queen of hearts, which we cover.

Declarer wins the trick with the ace of hearts and plays a spade, taken by Eric's nine. When Eric then plays a second heart, declarer loses his concentration and puts in the nine. We are therefore able to win with the ten of hearts and return a third round of the suit for Eric to ruff. We still have a club and two trump tricks to come.

The contract has rather unexpectedly gone four down: plus 800 to the good guys. This is a double whammy since the Canadians could have scored a similar number in the other direction by stopping to double us in Three Hearts.

This is the full deal:

$\spadesuit$ A 10 7 3 2
$\heartsuit$ A 8 5
$\diamond$ A 6
$\clubsuit$ A K 7

$\spadesuit$ 8
$\heartsuit$ K 10 6 3 2
$\diamond$ 2
$\clubsuit$ Q J 9 6 5 4

$\spadesuit$ K Q J 9 5
$\heartsuit$ 7 4
$\diamond$ Q J 9 7 4
$\clubsuit$ 3

$\spadesuit$ 6 4
$\heartsuit$ Q J 9
$\diamond$ K 10 8 5 3
$\clubsuit$ 10 8 2

At the other table, our teammates also allow East-West to escape, choosing instead to play in a failing **three notrump**. That is still a 13-IMP swing on the deal, though, leveling the momentum in the early stages.

The boards go quiet after the early excitement, but our hand on the final deal of the set has potential. With neither side vulnerable and LHO the dealer, we pick up:

$\spadesuit$ 9 $\heartsuit$ 5 4 2 $\diamond$ K 6 5 $\clubsuit$ A K Q 10 7 4

Gitelman opens with a strong (15-17) **one notrump**, and Eric comes in with a **two diamond** overcall — diamonds and a major. I am wondering how to investigate our best game when Mittelman surprises me with a jump to **three notrump**.

What do you make of this?

Fred Gitelman with Eric and Jeff

Eric clearly has a weakish distributional hand. We could compete to Four Diamonds or investigate a red-suit game, but the third option looks best — to **double** and defend. It takes some time for the bidding tray to come back from the other side of the screen, but eventually everyone passes. This has been the brief but explosive auction:

WEST	NORTH	EAST	SOUTH
Us	Gitelman	Eric	Mittelman
	1NT	2◊[1]	3NT
dbl	all pass		

1.   Diamonds and a major.

This was the full deal:

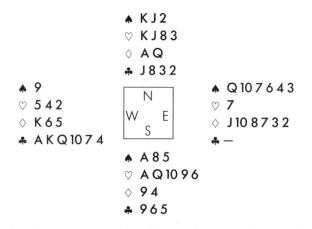

```
                    ♠ K J 2
                    ♡ K J 8 3
                    ◊ A Q
                    ♣ J 8 3 2
  ♠ 9                              ♠ Q 10 7 6 4 3
  ♡ 5 4 2             N            ♡ 7
  ◊ K 6 5         W     E          ◊ J 10 8 7 3 2
  ♣ A K Q 10 7 4      S            ♣ —
                    ♠ A 8 5
                    ♡ A Q 10 9 6
                    ◊ 9 4
                    ♣ 9 6 5
```

As it happens, the winning option would have been to bid Four Diamonds. The opponents would then have had a choice between doubling for plus 300 or trying Four Hearts, a contract that is likely to fail if played from the long trump hand (four rounds of clubs kills the spade discard on the jack of clubs).

Against Three Notrump Doubled, Eric leads his singleton heart, expecting that we would hold at least four cards in that suit and hoping that our double had 'find my suit' implications. Gitelman wins in dummy and immediately leads a club. We win with the queen of clubs and switch to a diamond, but the writing is on the wall when declarer's queen wins the trick.

We defend accurately and save the overtrick, but minus 550 does not look like a good score on a deal where our teammates are quite likely to go minus by playing game in their nine-card major-suit fit.

Indeed, they are well on their way to doing exactly that, but the Canadians sacrifice in Five Diamonds. The defenders lead trumps early, thus ensuring two spade tricks to go with their three red-suit winners. Our teammates are a little disappointed to lose 2 IMPs for their plus 500 but we are delighted to discover that the swing on the deal is that small.

We emerge from the first stanza with a small lead (34-25) but there is a very long way to go yet.

Jeff and Shirlee Meckstroth

Eric and I take a break for the second segment.

As I have said before, if we are going to sit out, we always prefer that it be early in a long match. I am hopeful that we won't sit out again — it's much easier (on the nerves) to be playing when the match is tight going into the final stages. In reality, though, this is likely to be our last break unless our lead gets into three figures.

As I've mentioned before, both Eric and I hate to watch the Vugraph. So, Eric has found a ballroom in the hotel that is usually empty, and he goes off to relax in his favorite manner — playing the piano. Meanwhile, I estimate that the time difference should enable me to catch the early stages of today's play in the Open Golf on ESPN. The disadvantage is that the Vugraph is also being shown on the television in my room and it is impossible not to check it from time to time.

The four-segments per day schedule means that both today and tomorrow the short break between sessions two and three will fall part way between lunchtime and a normal dinner hour. I therefore elect to take lunch in my room while watching the golf. I just hope I don't see anything to choke on when I check the Vugraph channel.

We return to the lobby outside the playing area two hours later, in plenty of time to join our team for the score comparison. As it happens, the boards were relatively dull during this segment. We tag on another 8 IMPs, winning the stanza 31-23.

Eric relaxes

Final: Set Three
Running Score: USA 65 — Canada 48

We go into the Open Room for this set, against Eric Kokish and Joey Silver. This is a very dangerous pair. Both are veterans and all-round good guys. Kokish (I won't call him Eric too, because that will get very confusing) is a tremendous theoretician and he has helped our team greatly in the role of coach. For the duration of this match, though, we can forget the friendship — it'll be a war!

On the first deal of the set, with both sides vulnerable and Eric the dealer, we pick up this interesting collection:

♠ K Q 10 9 6 3 2 ♡ — ◇ A 10 3 2 ♣ 4 2

Eric opens **one heart** and we respond in our long suit — **one spade**. When Eric then rebids **two clubs**, our prospects for anything higher than game are remote. Indeed, we may not even have a game, but I am never not bidding one.

I do not see how anything can be gained by advancing slowly from here, so let's bid what we think/hope we can make — **four spades**. The auction has been straightforward:

WEST	NORTH	EAST	SOUTH
Silver	Eric	Kokish	Us
	1♡	pass	1♠
pass	2♣	pass	4♠
all pass			

Silver leads the five of diamonds (third and fifth) and Eric produces a fairly average dummy:

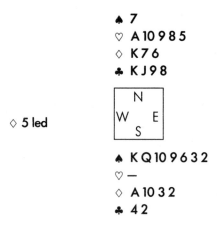

♠ 7
♡ A 10 9 8 5
◇ K 7 6
♣ K J 9 8

◇ 5 led

```
    N
  W   E
    S
```

♠ K Q 10 9 6 3 2
♡ —
◇ A 10 3 2
♣ 4 2

The opening lead goes to East's diamond queen and we win with the ace. **How would you continue?**

One option is to play a diamond to the king, pitch a diamond on the ace of hearts, and then try to guess the black suits.

As a general principle, it is usually best to leave guesses until as late in the hand as possible, so that you can collect information that will help you guess right more often than not. However, our chances here may be improved by leading a club at Trick 2.

Although it has become almost routine to follow low in tempo when declarer leads towards a king-jack combination, every defender knows that there are layouts on which it is right to rise with the ace. If Silver holds the ace he may rise with it. Most important, though, are the hands on which West holds both the ace and the queen of clubs. Then he will certainly rise with the ace and we will score two club tricks by putting in the jack on the second round. We can then pitch diamonds on the heart ace and dummy's second club winner and score plus 620 even if there are two trump losers.

Even if the club honors are split and we guess wrong, we are still not down. If East wins and returns a club, he establishes a second diamond discard for us, and then we will just have to guess the trumps. If, instead, he returns a second diamond, we can then pitch our second club on the ace of hearts and play for diamonds 3-3 and a winning trump guess.

Playing a club immediately looks best both on psychological and technical grounds.

As expected, West follows low on the club. We therefore call for dummy's jack, which forces East's ace. Kokish returns a diamond to dummy's king and we pitch our fourth diamond on the ace of hearts. All that remains now is to guess trumps, and the percentage play is to finesse against the jack.

A trump to the ten loses to West's ace and he cashes his diamond winner. When trumps subsequently divide 3-2, we can claim ten tricks; plus 620.

This is the full hand:

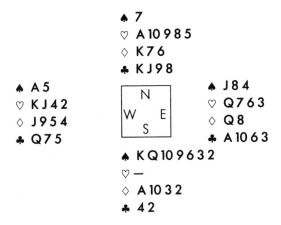

The contract and the opening lead were the same at the other table. The Canadian declarer crossed to the diamond king and took a diamond discard straight away. He then finessed in trumps and subsequently guessed the clubs to bring home his contract.

After a string of relatively uninteresting boards, we are dealt a hand with plenty of potential as the stanza draws to a close. With only our side vulnerable, and LHO the dealer, we pick up:

♠ A K J 6 5 4 3 ♡ A Q 8 2 ◇ 6 ♣ 5

Joey Silver opens **one diamond**, which is followed by two passes around to us.

How do you assess the various options?

The realistic choices are a jump to Four Spades or a takeout double. (Two Diamonds would be Michaels, but we play that as 5-5, so it's not an option here.) Despite the obvious danger of partner passing, I feel that **double** is the better choice — after all, we could easily belong in hearts at the four- or even the six-level.

Silver continues with **two clubs** and Eric bids **two diamonds** — a cuebid showing decent values in a hand that does not want to commit to any particular suit or level. RHO jumps to **four diamonds** now, but that doesn't hinder us — we were going to bid **four spades** anyway.

Things get a little trickier when Silver advances to **five diamonds** and Eric **doubles**, saying 'let's defend.'

We have three options now — pass partner's double, advance to Five Spades, or make a slam try with Five Hearts. **Which would you choose?**

If partner wants to defend Five Diamonds Doubled, the chances that we have a slam are remote, so let's rule out Five Hearts and concentrate on the 'play or defend' decision. We really wish they had let us have it in Four Spades, but we don't need much from Eric to make eleven tricks. Our 'best case' scenario defending is probably going to be plus 300, and possibly worse, so I think it's worth the risk to try for the vulnerable game bonus. We settle for **five spades** and everyone passes.

WEST	NORTH	EAST	SOUTH
Silver	*Eric*	*Kokish*	*Us*
1◇	pass	pass	dbl
2♣	2◇	4◇	4♠
5◇	dbl	pass	5♠
all pass			

This is the full deal:

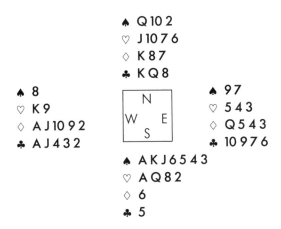

```
                    ♠ Q 10 2
                    ♡ J 10 7 6
                    ◇ K 8 7
                    ♣ K Q 8
     ♠ 8                             ♠ 9 7
     ♡ K 9          N                ♡ 5 4 3
     ◇ A J 10 9 2  W   E             ◇ Q 5 4 3
     ♣ A J 4 3 2      S              ♣ 10 9 7 6
                    ♠ A K J 6 5 4 3
                    ♡ A Q 8 2
                    ◇ 6
                    ♣ 5
```

With the heart finesse failing, even Five Spades might have been too high, let alone the slam that we were considering trying for, albeit briefly. Fortunately, though, West also holds both minor-suit aces, and thus the defense can never come to more than two tricks. It is rare for values such as dummy holds in the minors to be of so much use offensively when they are facing two singletons.

At the other table, our teammates buy the contract in Five Clubs Doubled. They lose the obvious five tricks; minus 500. We therefore pick up 4 IMPs on the deal.

We win the third segment 35-29, padding our lead by 6 IMPs. After three hotly contested sets, we have built a 23-IMP advantage going into the final stanza of the first day.

We remain in the Open Room for the last set of the day, this time against the 'Men' — Mittelman-Gitelman.

The set starts poorly — first we under-compete on a partscore hand and then we give declarer an easy ride in a tight game contract when he probably would have taken a wrong view on a more testing defense.

Nearing the midway point of the set, with only our side vulnerable and Eric the dealer, we pick up:

♠ A K Q 4 ♡ 10 4 3 ◇ Q 6 5 ♣ A Q 7

Eric gets things rolling with a nebulous **one diamond** opening and we make the obvious **one spade** response. Eric raises this to **two spades**, which promises four trumps but also shows a minimum opening bid and specifically denies a singleton anywhere — he could have made a mini-splinter with a distributional hand.

In this situation we play Three Clubs as an artificial game try, while Three Diamonds shows slam interest. We are just about worth a slam try — he could have something like

♠ J x x x ♡ A x ◇ A K x x x ♣ J x

Opener's first priority over Three Diamonds, though, is to establish the quality of the trump suit. In this case, since we hold all of the top honors, we know that Eric will bid 3NT (denying a top spade). We cannot, therefore, find out anything useful below the four-level and with two balanced hands there is a risk of getting overboard.

I hate to go down in a slam — I would much rather be wrong by missing a slam than by going down in one. In general, we tend to ignore slams that require partner to hold a perfect hand — he rarely does — in favor of concealing information from the opponents.

It is certainly conceivable that even game will not be cold here, so the unrevealing jump to **four spades** looks like the best option.

WEST	NORTH	EAST	SOUTH
Gitelman	*Eric*	*Mittelman*	*Us*
	1◇	pass	1♠
pass	2♠	pass	4♠
all pass			

West leads the nine of hearts and Eric puts down a fairly decent dummy in the context of the auction:

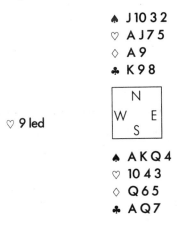

♠ J 10 3 2
♡ A J 7 5
◇ A 9
♣ K 9 8

♡ 9 led

♠ A K Q 4
♡ 10 4 3
◇ Q 6 5
♣ A Q 7

We duck the opening lead to East's heart queen and win the trump return. A second round of spades reveals that the suit breaks evenly, so we draw a third round of trumps, play a heart to the ace, and exit with a third heart to East's king.

East gets out with a club, so we concede a diamond and claim ten tricks.

I see that East started with the king of diamonds and only three hearts to the king-queen. If I had cashed my clubs before playing the third heart, he would have been endplayed to concede an eleventh trick. Too bad — conservation of energy is very important in long tournaments. My belief is that overtricks are not important in long IMP matches. Even if you lose by 1 IMP, it wasn't an overtrick, it was because of all the big swings you lost. Speed of play is also a factor — playing slowly makes it more difficult to maintain concentration when it really matters. I am much more likely to lose an overtrick in a cold contract than to take a long time and expend my mental energy in order to make the extra trick.

With just a handful of boards left in the day, Eric deals with both sides vulnerable and we pick up:

♠ J 10 9 8 3 ♡ K ◇ K 7 5 3 ♣ K 4 3

George Mittelman and Dianna Gordon

The auction starts with two passes. Any thoughts?

I always try to bid in third seat if I can. No matter what system you play, bidding in third seat will reap dividends. Doing so puts the opponents into a defensive bidding situation, which automatically reduces their options. (They can no longer open Two Notrump or Two Clubs, over which they no doubt have a well-oiled system for reaching the best contract, for example.) Some players might choose to open a hand like this with a weak two-bid, but I prefer not to open Two Spades if I fear being in Two Spades Doubled as a contract, so my third-seat weak twos tend to be quite sound.

We therefore elect to open **one spade** and LHO overcalls this with **one notrump**. After a pass from Eric, Mittelman tries Stayman, **two clubs**, and Gitelman jumps to **three hearts**, showing a maximum with five hearts. This is raised to **four hearts** and everyone passes.

WEST	NORTH	EAST	SOUTH
Gitelman	Eric	Mittelman	Us
	pass	pass	1♠
1NT	pass	2♣	pass
3♡	pass	4♡	all pass

Eric leads the nine of clubs and George tables a fair dummy. This is the full deal:

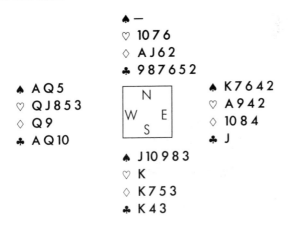

```
                    ♠ —
                    ♡ 10 7 6
                    ◊ A J 6 2
                    ♣ 9 8 7 6 5 2
  ♠ A Q 5                              ♠ K 7 6 4 2
  ♡ Q J 8 5 3          N              ♡ A 9 4 2
  ◊ Q 9            W       E          ◊ 10 8 4
  ♣ A Q 10              S             ♣ J
                    ♠ J 10 9 8 3
                    ♡ K
                    ◊ K 7 5 3
                    ♣ K 4 3
```

The effect of two weeks hard concentration is obviously beginning to take its toll, as I cover dummy's jack of clubs at Trick 1. Declarer promptly discards two diamonds on his club winners and plays a trump to dummy's ace. When our king falls, Gitelman claims twelve tricks; minus 680. Withholding the king of clubs would have saved the second overtrick.

As it happens, though, it is Fred's decision to overcall 1NT that proves to be the critical decision on the deal. At the other table, South also opened One Spade but our West elected to start with a takeout double. East responded in hearts, so the same contract was reached, but with our hand on lead. The Canadian

South, naturally enough, led the jack of spades, and was well rewarded when North ruffed. Two rounds of diamonds put South back on lead and a second spade ruff defeated the game.

We lose a fairly random 13 IMPs on this deal which, although we don't know it at the time, puts the Canadians ahead briefly for the first time in the match.

When we meet with our teammates to score the fourth stanza, neither pair is happy with their card. We lose the stanza 36-14, which leaves us with the lead in the match, but by only the narrowest of margins. We are all still in good spirits, though. We are a very practical team — we know we cannot win every set. It's all about outscoring them at the end. We retire to the bar for a quick drink while we discuss our general plans for the next day's play. Slightly more than half of the Bermuda Bowl final remains and battle has been truly joined — the overnight score is USA 114 — Canada 113.

Fred Gitelman

We are back in the Open Room at the start of the second day's play in the final. Our opponents are Boris Baran and Mark Molson. This is the first time we have seen Baran-Molson but, as expected at the outset, they have played very well against our teammates.

The day starts with two flat-looking game hands. Then, with both sides vulnerable, we deal and pick up:

♠ K 10 ♡ K 10 4 ◊ A 7 6 ♣ K 8 6 4 3

The lack of intermediates in the club suit means that this hand is not good enough to upgrade to a 14-16 notrump, and we therefore start proceedings with a nebulous **one diamond** opening. Eric responds **one spade** and Baran enters the fray with a **two hearts** overcall.

We play support doubles in this position, so our **pass** now suggests a relatively balanced hand (no Three Clubs or Three Diamonds rebid) with a maximum of two spades. Molson also **passes** and Eric re-opens with a **double. What would you do?**

We play Eric's double as showing enough high-card values for me to pass with four decent trumps. Passing without a fourth trump is far too risky, though, so that's not an option. Retreating to Three Clubs or Two Notrump is too pessimistic for me — with an absolute maximum (having not opened a 14-16 notrump) and a five-card suit, you have to try for game. We therefore jump to **three notrump**.

WEST	NORTH	EAST	SOUTH
Molson	Eric	Baran	Us
			1◊
pass	1♠	2♡	pass
pass	dbl	pass	3NT
all pass			

West leads the jack of diamonds and Eric displays a fairly minimum dummy:

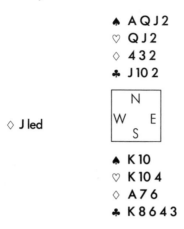

♠ A Q J 2
♡ Q J 2
◊ 4 3 2
♣ J 10 2

N
W   E
S

◊ J led

♠ K 10
♡ K 10 4
◊ A 7 6
♣ K 8 6 4 3

We have both stretched slightly, so it is hardly a surprise that the contract is not great. Having said that, I am not upset at being in an odds-against game. I've been in far worse. It's just a case of finding a layout that will allow us to make nine tricks and then playing on the assumption that it exists.

East overtakes with the diamond queen at Trick 1 and we let him win. We duck again when he continues with the king of diamonds. Things start to look up when he then switches to ace and another heart (West discarding a spade on the second round). **Where should we win this trick?**

We are going to have to do something with the clubs, and we may need a late entry to dummy, so let's get the king of hearts out of the way by winning with it now. We then cash three rounds of spades, throwing a club from hand on the third as East pitches a heart.

We have only seven tricks, so we are going to need the club suit to produce two more. Finding the ace of clubs onside will not help, so we must play East for the club queen. We therefore lead the jack of clubs, and run it when East follows with a low card.

West wins with the ace of clubs and exits with the ten of diamonds, on which East throws another heart. We win the ace of diamonds, enter dummy with the queen of hearts and cash our fourth spade trick. All that now remains is to guess the two-card ending.

If East's last two cards are ♣Q-9, we can do nothing. The important cases are when East now has the bare queen of clubs and when West has the singleton nine remaining. A simple count tells us which of these options to play for — East started with six hearts, two diamonds and two spades; thus, he also began with three clubs. A quick check confirms that West was originally 5-1-5-2. Our only chance is that West's remaining club is the nine. We therefore lead the ten of clubs. East covers with the queen and West's nine falls under our king. The eight of clubs is our ninth winner at Trick 13.

The full hand is:

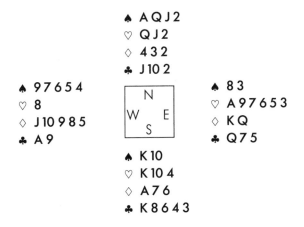

```
                    ♠ A Q J 2
                    ♡ Q J 2
                    ◇ 4 3 2
                    ♣ J 10 2
  ♠ 9 7 6 5 4          N          ♠ 8 3
  ♡ 8            W         E       ♡ A 9 7 6 5 3
  ◇ J 10 9 8 5          S         ◇ K Q
  ♣ A 9                            ♣ Q 7 5
                    ♠ K 10
                    ♡ K 10 4
                    ◇ A 7 6
                    ♣ K 8 6 4 3
```

At the other table, the Canadian North declares Three Clubs and he misguesses the trumps to go one down. A 12-IMP swing to get the ball rolling this morning. Indeed, as the set progresses we build up quite a head of steam. Momentum is an important thing — if it feels like things are going well, you tend to play better. You also tend to get the rub of the green, while every close decision the opponents make seems to work out poorly for them. Towards the end of this stanza, we seem to be playing in what Zia would call 'Heat One', where everything we do works.

Mark Molson

The stanza is a virtual whitewash: we win it 58-9 to lead by an even 50 IMPs at the halfway point in the match. To suffer such a reversal immediately after fighting their way back into a match would spell the end for many teams. Now we'll get a chance to see just how good this Canadian sextet is. Will they roll over and die or will they come back fighting? If I had to bet, I'd say this match was still far from over, but one more big set will surely seal it for us.

Eric and I return to the Open Room with the wind in our sails. Our opponents for this segment are Mittelman-Gitelman.

Early in the set, with only the opponents vulnerable and Eric the dealer, we pick up:

♠ A K 6   ♡ 10 9 6 4 2   ◇ K 6 5 4   ♣ 9

Eric kicks things off with a strong, artificial **one club** and we respond **one spade**, showing positive values (8+ HCP) with at least five hearts, and forcing to game.

Eric bids **two diamonds** (showing clubs) and we respond **two hearts**, saying nothing more about hearts, but denying a club fit and showing extra values.

Eric's **three hearts** bid now sets that suit as trumps and we co-operate with a **three spades** cuebid. Eric now bids **three notrump** — a 'serious' slam try. **How good is our hand, do you think?**

In the context of what we have already shown, it is about as poor as it could be, despite the good controls. We have shown 8+ HCP and then extra values, so we can hardly have fewer high cards. We also have a terrible suit and a singleton in partner's main suit. The most discouraging bid at this point is **four hearts**, which is what we choose, and everyone passes.

Tiananmen Square

WEST	NORTH	EAST	SOUTH
Gitelman	*Eric*	*Mittelman*	*Us*
	1♣[1]	pass	1♠[2]
pass	2◊[3]	pass	2♡[4]
pass	3♡[5]	pass	3♠[6]
pass	3NT[7]	pass	4♡
all pass			

1. Strong, artificial.
2. Shows hearts with 8+ HCP.
3. Shows clubs.
4. No club fit, but extra values (!).
5. Agrees hearts.
6. Cuebid.
7. Serious slam try.

Fred Gitelman leads the nine of diamonds and Eric produces a fair dummy:

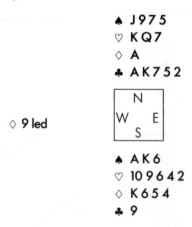

♠ J 9 7 5
♡ K Q 7
◊ A
♣ A K 7 5 2

◊ 9 led

♠ A K 6
♡ 10 9 6 4 2
◊ K 6 5 4
♣ 9

This looks like a straightforward hand but it is important to play carefully just in case there are bad breaks around.

As we will probably want to ruff a diamond in dummy, there is nothing to be gained by leading trumps towards dummy's honors. **Should we therefore lead a high trump from dummy at Trick 2?**

That would probably work, but perhaps we can do better by not touching trumps at all. We can pitch our losing spade on dummy's second club winner and plan to ruff both small diamonds. That seems best...

We win the ace of diamonds, cash the ace-king of clubs for a spade discard, play a spade to the ace, take the king of diamonds, and lead a third diamond. LHO pitches a club on this trick, so we ruff with the heart seven and cross to the king of spades. When we then play a fourth diamond, LHO shrugs and pitches the queen of spades.

We ruff with the queen and lead the king of hearts. RHO pitches a spade on this trick — so West began with all five trumps. There is nothing he can do now, though. In fact, he allows the heart king to win. We already have nine tricks and we must make one more with our 10-9-6-4 of trumps.

At the other table, our West led a low spade at Trick 1, and dummy's jack won. With only one diamond to ruff, declarer could now afford to lead the king of hearts from the dummy. This revealed the bad news in trumps, but with careful play he was still able to arrive at ten tricks: a push board at plus 420.

Even at this level, the opponents do not always find the most testing defense. With neither side vulnerable and LHO the dealer, we pick up:

♠ Q864 ♡ K5 ◇ KJ983 ♣ A8

Eric opens a catch-all **one diamond** in second seat and Mittelman comes in with a **two clubs** overcall. We have a choice here — an inverted, forcing Two Diamonds or a negative double. **Do you have any thoughts?**

> A negative double here should really promise both majors and one needs to be very careful when using it without them. You must be prepared to handle auctions when partner bids the major you don't hold. Of course, there is less risk playing a Strong Club system, since partner cannot have a very big hand. On this deal, with a relatively balanced hand, we decide it is safe to **double**, checking for a spade fit, and intending to bid Three Notrump if we don't find one.

Gitelman raises to **three clubs** and Eric **doubles**, which we play as showing four-card support for both majors. Mittelman tries to crowd the auction with a preemptive push to **four clubs**, but that does us no harm as we were going to bid **four spades** anyway. LHO's **double** concludes an eventful auction:

WEST	NORTH	EAST	SOUTH
Gitelman	*Eric*	*Mittelman*	*Us*
pass	1◊	2♣	dbl
3♣	dbl¹	4♣	4♠
dbl	all pass		

1. Four-card support for both majors.

West leads the jack of clubs and Eric unveils a dummy with little in the way of spare values:

```
              ♠ A K 10 9
              ♡ Q 9 8 4
              ◊ Q 7 5
              ♣ 7 3
                 ┌─────┐
                 │  N  │
   ♣ J led       │ W  E│
                 │  S  │
                 └─────┘
              ♠ Q 8 6 4
              ♡ K 5
              ◊ K J 9 8 3
              ♣ A 8
```

West's double strongly suggests that the trumps will break 5-0. With the risk of being forced in clubs a live possibility, it looks right to set about establishing our diamonds while we still have plenty of options in the trump suit. We therefore lead the king of diamonds from hand at Trick 2.

East takes this with the ace of diamonds, cashes a club, and exits with a second round of diamonds, West following. Now is the time to start trumps and, when we cash the ace, East surprises us a little by following suit. He shows out when we play a second trump to our queen, but we are in control now. We need to score a heart trick, and we must do that now, before drawing the rest of the trumps, so we lead the king from hand.

West takes the ace of hearts and exits with a third round of diamonds, severing our link in that suit. However, we can use the diamond winners as trump substitutes now — we simply keep leading winning diamonds to trap West's trump holding. He can ruff in, but we will then overruff, draw the last trump, and ruff a heart to hand to cash the long diamond. If West discards, then we will throw a heart loser from dummy and lead the fifth diamond to repeat the process.

The whole deal:

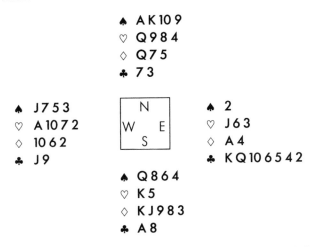

```
              ♠ A K 10 9
              ♡ Q 9 8 4
              ◇ Q 7 5
              ♣ 7 3
  ♠ J 7 5 3        N        ♠ 2
  ♡ A 10 7 2   W       E    ♡ J 6 3
  ◇ 10 6 2         S        ◇ A 4
  ♣ J 9                     ♣ K Q 10 6 5 4 2
              ♠ Q 8 6 4
              ♡ K 5
              ◇ K J 9 8 3
              ♣ A 8
```

Had West's minor-suit shape been reversed, the defense would have prevailed here. With West holding the long diamond, though, we could always make the hand provided we timed it correctly.

Even as the cards lie, the defenders could have given us a much rougher ride. Suppose the king of diamonds had been allowed to hold Trick 2, for example. We would then have to read the distribution well to prevail. Even having won the ace of diamonds on the first round, East would have done better to cash his club winner and then play a third club, giving a ruff and discard. Again, we can still make the contract if we read everything well, but that defense would give us far more chances to go wrong.

As a defender, you can often see that declarer is destined to make his contract. That is no reason to give up, though. Look for a way to give him a guess. Make him work for every trick.

Most opponents are well aware that Eric and I like to bid. You should always be looking to double thin games if suits are breaking badly or you can see honors are badly placed for declarer, and this is particularly true when your opponents are known to be very aggressive bidders. However, West's double on this hand was a little too much — apart from the 4-1 trump split, the defense just did not have enough material.

Indeed, people do like to double Meckwell — they all know how aggressive we are. However, when you double a good declarer, you alert him to bad splits and, in many cases, this allows him to play the hand a trick better. Eric and I do not tend to double a lot. It seems to us that they go down when we don't double but that when we do they frequently make. We rarely lose IMPs when we simply beat them in their aggressive contracts.

Don't forget that you're already gaining 5 or 6 IMPs for plus 50 or plus 100 when teammates have plus 140. The double gains only one or two extra IMPs, or maybe an extra 4 IMPs when the contract goes two down. If your double tips declarer off to the winning line, and turns plus 100 into minus

790, that's an 18-IMP swing (the 6 you would have gained plus the 12 you now lose). For these close doubles to show a substantial profit, you need at lot of small swings to compensate for the odd large one in the minus column.

At the other table, South also declared Four Spades. The defense there was also not overly testing, so he scored up his contract. This time, therefore, the double costs 5 IMPs.

The Canadians win the sixth set, but only by one IMP, 35-34. At the meal break on the second day of the final, we lead by 49 with just sixty-four boards remaining.

Irving Litvack, Canadian npc

Final: Set Seven
Running Score: USA 206 — Canada 157

For the penultimate stanza of the second day, Eric and I return to the Open Room, this time against Kokish and Silver.

With both sides vulnerable and Eric the dealer, we pick up:

♠ A J 10 7 3   ♡ —   ◊ A J 9 7   ♣ 10 8 7 3

After a pass from Eric, Kokish opens **one club** on our right and it looks clear for us to overcall **one spade**. Silver makes a non-constructive raise to **two clubs** and Eric joins in with **two spades**, which Kokish **passes**.

Where are the hearts? We have a 10-count and Eric could only raise to Two Spades. We are surely outgunned. Is it possible that the opponents can make Four Hearts despite the 4-0 or 5-0 trump break? Unlikely, but possible. To kill any chance of LHO backing in with a double and uncovering their major-suit fit it seems right to make an obstructive raise to **three spades**.

WEST	NORTH	EAST	SOUTH
Silver	Eric	Kokish	Us
	pass	1♣	1♠
2♣	2♠	pass	3♠
all pass			

West leads the two of hearts and Eric puts down a dummy with enough defensive values that we need not have worried about the opponents making a game:

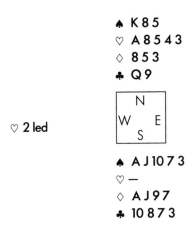

```
              ♠ K 8 5
              ♡ A 8 5 4 3
              ◇ 8 5 3
              ♣ Q 9
                 ┌─────┐
                 │  N  │
   ♡ 2 led     W │     │ E
                 │  S  │
                 └─────┘
              ♠ A J 10 7 3
              ♡ —
              ◇ A J 9 7
              ♣ 10 8 7 3
```

Having hoisted ourselves to the three-level, unnecessarily as it turns out, we have our work cut out. It looks right to play low from dummy and ruff in hand at Trick 1. We then lead a club to the nine and East's king. Kokish returns a trump and, when we put in the ten, West follows with the nine.

We then lead the ten of clubs (remember, West knows we have the ten because his partner captured the nine with the king on the first round) to the queen and ace. We win the trump return in hand with the jack, West pitching a heart. We then lead the seven of clubs and run it, throwing a heart from dummy when West does not cover with the jack.

Now we can see a way home — ruff the fourth round of clubs with the king of spades, cash the ace of heart throwing a diamond, cross to the ace of diamonds, and exit with a diamond. We must then score the ace and the seven of spades at the end.

This is the full deal:

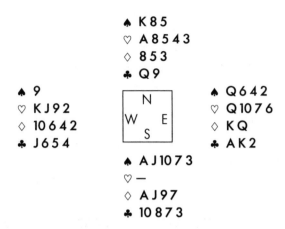

```
              ♠ K 8 5
              ♡ A 8 5 4 3
              ◇ 8 5 3
              ♣ Q 9
♠ 9                           ♠ Q 6 4 2
♡ K J 9 2          N          ♡ Q 10 7 6
◇ 10 6 4 2     W     E        ◇ K Q
♣ J 6 5 4          S          ♣ A K 2
              ♠ A J 10 7 3
              ♡ —
              ◇ A J 9 7
              ♣ 10 8 7 3
```

Should West have covered the seven of clubs with the jack on the third round? Yes, and of course he would have done so if he was wide awake, but two solid weeks of concentration take their toll.

He might have asked himself why we had made a point of showing him the ten of clubs on the second round, but such questions are much easier to answer when sitting at home reading about the hand. Of course, if we had held only ♣10-7-3, and we had just played them randomly, it would not have cost him to cover either.

Tiny lapses in concentration can cost a bundle of points at this level, and those 'little' 4-6 IMP swings can add up fast.

At the other table, our East opened with a strong notrump. The Canadian with my hand overcalled Two Spades and his partner raised to game. The defense was accurate and thus declarer went two down; plus 200. An 8-IMP gain on what was really a nothing board.

The final deal of the stanza is one guaranteed to wake up anyone in the Vugraph audience who has started to nod. With just our side vulnerable, we deal and pick up:

♠ A K 9 6   ♡ J 9 6 4   ◇ 5   ♣ K 8 4 2

We have a system bid for this hand — **two hearts**, which shows 11-15 HCP, a singleton diamond and 4-3 or 4-4 in the majors.

Silver passes and the bidding tray remains on the other side of the screen for a very long time. When it comes back through, it is clear why — Eric has jumped to **seven clubs** and Kokish has bid **seven diamonds**. So much for our reputation as scientific bidders!

In the context of our opening bid, we had quite a suitable hand for a high club contract. With no additional playing strength such as a fifth club and no stray minor honors, it is not nearly as good for a grand slam in notrump. A forcing pass would invite Eric to carry on, so we **double** and that concludes a most unusual auction.

WEST	NORTH	EAST	SOUTH
Silver	Eric	Kokish	Us
			2♡
pass	7♣	7◇	dbl
all pass			

This is the full hand:

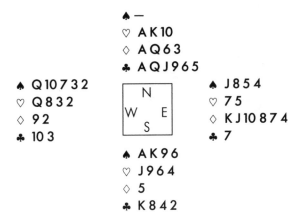

```
              ♠ —
              ♡ A K 10
              ◇ A Q 6 3
              ♣ A Q J 9 6 5
♠ Q 10 7 3 2      N        ♠ J 8 5 4
♡ Q 8 3 2     W       E    ♡ 7 5
◇ 9 2             S        ◇ K J 10 8 7 4
♣ 10 3                     ♣ 7
              ♠ A K 9 6
              ♡ J 9 6 4
              ◇ 5
              ♣ K 8 4 2
```

We lead the king of spades on which Eric discards a low club. We then play the nine of spades (reverse suit preference showing a high club) for Eric to ruff. He puts us back in with the king of clubs enabling us to cash the ace of spades and deliver a second spade ruff. After the ace and king of hearts, Eric puts declarer in his hand with a club ruff. Kokish tries the king of diamonds in the hope of collecting the singleton queen, but it is not to be and Eric scores two more trump tricks — nine down! This means a penalty of 2300 and a 4-IMP gain even if the Canadians bid their grand slam in the other room.

Kokish's decision to bid was not a bad shot, though. Assuming that our grand slam was making, and it seemed unlikely that Eric would have taken a wild stab at a grand slam in a match we were leading comfortably, Kokish did not need to make many tricks to show a profit.

Indeed, with the Canadians at the other table stopping in Six Clubs, Kokish's sacrifice costs only one IMP rather than four, as we gain 14 IMPs on the deal

The stanza goes well for us at both tables and we gain a further 26 IMPs (48-22). With just forty-eight deals to play, we are ahead by seventy-five — not quite cruising, but comfortable at least.

Eric Kokish

For the last set of the second day, we are back on Vugraph, this time against Baran-Molson, and they play extremely well against us. There are a handful of boards on which we will not be surprised to lose a double-figure swing.

Towards the end of the set, with both sides vulnerable, Eric deals and we pick up:

♠ 9 8 7 6 3　♡ J 6 4 3　◇ A　♣ J 10 4

Eric kicks off with a strong, artificial **one club** opening and Molson comes in with a **one heart** overcall. We have to start with a **double**, which is two-way — either a balanced positive with no heart stopper or most hands in the 5-7 HCP range.

Baran boosts the preempt to **three hearts** and Eric backs in with **four diamonds**, passed on our right. We now have a particularly nasty problem — we have to bid something as Four Diamonds is forcing. We do have two things going for us, though — we have already denied a decent six-card spade suit (Two Spades over One Heart would have shown 3-6 HCP and a fair six-card suit). Plus, with a decent five-card suit, our style is to stretch to bid One Spade even on slightly less than positive values, as doing so tends to simplify the later auction. We can therefore bid **four spades** now, knowing that Eric will not expect a particularly good suit. No one doubles, which is a good sign.

WEST	NORTH	EAST	SOUTH
Baran	Eric	Molson	Us
	1♣	1♡	dbl[1]
3♡	4◇	pass	4♠
all pass			

1. Balanced positive with no heart stopper or most 5-7 hands.

West leads the ace of hearts, and Eric puts down a rather motley collection in the circumstances.

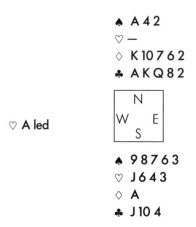

♠ A 4 2
♡ —
◇ K 10 7 6 2
♣ A K Q 8 2

♡ A led

N
W E
S

♠ 9 8 7 6 3
♡ J 6 4 3
◇ A
♣ J 10 4

We have two choices. We can simply play for a 3-2 trump break — ruff the opening lead, unblock the diamond ace, take a second heart ruff, cash the ace of spades, pitch a heart on the king of diamonds, cross back to the jack of clubs, and play a trump. If spades split 3-2, the defenders will get two trump tricks and a heart.

The other option is to try guarding against some 4-1 trump splits by playing on clubs. This will work if trumps are 3-2 or 4-1, provided the defender with the short trumps does not also have short clubs. Even if clubs are 4-1, we will still be okay provided the defender with the singleton also holds the spade length.

Would someone have doubled Four Spades if he held a strong four-card trump holding? Perhaps, but that is less than clear when doing so might frighten us into an alternative, making, contract such as Five Clubs.

The second line looks like the better option, so we ruff the opening heart lead, unblock the diamond ace, and then play three rounds of clubs. LHO ruffs the third round and returns a diamond. We rise with the king, pitching a heart from hand, ruff a diamond, ruff a heart with dummy's second low trump, and cash the ace of spades.

We now lead a fourth round of clubs from dummy, discarding the last heart loser from our hand. The defenders can score their remaining trumps separately — we have lost three trump tricks but that is all. Now take a look at the full deal:

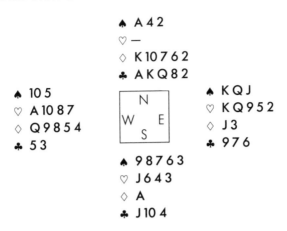

                    ♠ A 4 2
                    ♡ —
                    ◇ K 10 7 6 2
                    ♣ A K Q 8 2

    ♠ 10 5   ♠ K Q J
    ♡ A 10 8 7   N   ♡ K Q 9 5 2
    ◇ Q 9 8 5 4   W   E   ◇ J 3
    ♣ 5 3   S   ♣ 9 7 6

                    ♠ 9 8 7 6 3
                    ♡ J 6 4 3
                    ◇ A
                    ♣ J 10 4

Do you notice anything?

The defender with the short clubs also had short trumps!

As the cards lie, we chose the wrong line of play, but we were allowed to get away with it. Had West returned a trump after ruffing the third round of clubs, East would have been able to ruff in on the third round of diamonds and draw dummy's third trump before we had taken a second heart ruff. The defense would then score three trumps and a heart for one down.

At the other table, the Canadians stop in a club partscore, making ten tricks; minus 130. Our plus 620 therefore translates into a 10-IMP gain on the board. West had the chance to gain 6 IMPs for his side once we had chosen the wrong option in the play. At this late stage of the match, a 16-IMP reduction in the margin would have made a considerable difference, at least psychologically.

Attentive readers will have noticed that on most deals where we have more than the balance of the HCP, by however slight a margin, even with only a very moderate trump fit, as here, Eric and I tend to bid game. This has always been our style, and I believe it is the right one — defense is by far the most difficult part of the game, even for the best players. In this book, you have seen some of the top players in the world slip and let through a game that should have been defeated. Indeed, I have made a point of including plenty of hands on which errors were made (by both sides) to illustrate that players at this level do not play perfectly. To do so is not possible. What is important is that you do not let an error on one deal affect your concentration on the next. It is also vital that you take advantage when the opponents make a slip, which is something that West failed to do on the previous deal.

Boris Baran

The Canucks win the final stanza of the day by 42-34, cutting our overall advantage to 67 IMPs with just 32 boards remaining — a considerable advantage. We will go to bed and sleep fairly comfortably tonight.

Indeed, it must seem to spectators, both those watching on the Vugraph here in China and to those following the action around the world via the internet, that the outcome of the final is now a virtual certainty. As we are to find out tomorrow, though, no one thought to tell the Canadians this.

We are again on Vugraph for the first stanza of the championship's final day. Our opponents are Molson-Baran, who played well against us last night. They do so again this morning, and midway through the stanza, with both sides vulnerable and LHO the dealer, we pick up:

♠ — ♡ 10 9 8 6 3 ◇ K Q 7 ♣ Q 9 7 6 2

Eric opens a nebulous **one diamond** in second seat, we respond **one heart**, and Molson enters with a **one spade** overcall. Eric makes a Support **double**, showing three hearts, and Baran shows a sound spade raise with a **two hearts** cuebid.

It sounds as if the points are fairly evenly split, but we have some extra distributional values so we are prepared to compete to the three-level. We play a **three hearts** bid in this situation as purely competitive, showing extra shape but not invitational, so that's our choice.

It is not a surprise when Molson continues to **three spades**. What is unexpected is to hear Eric bid again, with **four diamonds**. Clearly he has a hand with extra distribution too.

We haven't climbed to the four-level to play in a partscore, so it seems right to correct to **four hearts**. Thus ends a fairly unconvincing auction:

WEST	NORTH	EAST	SOUTH
Molson	*Eric*	*Baran*	*Us*
pass	1◇	pass	1♡
1♠	dbl¹	2♡	3♡
3♠	4◇	pass	4♡
all pass			

1. Three-card heart support

Molson leads the jack of clubs and Eric puts down a fair hand:

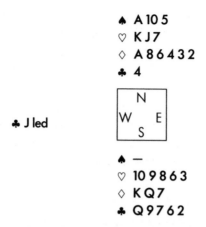

♠ A 10 5
♡ K J 7
◇ A 8 6 4 3 2
♣ 4

♣ J led

♠ —
♡ 10 9 8 6 3
◇ K Q 7
♣ Q 9 7 6 2

Here we are again in game with only an eight-card fit and this time less than half of the high cards! Not that the contract is a hopeless one — far from it: if the trumps break we are odds-on to make ten tricks.

East wins Trick 1 with the king of clubs and returns a spade. As we want to start trumps from hand, we ruff the spade. We then lead the ten of hearts and run it, losing to East's queen.

Baran returns a second spade and again we ruff in hand to lead a trump. West rises with the ace but, when East follows suit, we are just about home. Molson plays a club, but we ruff with the king of hearts, cross to hand in diamonds, and draw the last trump with the nine of hearts. Dummy is now high.

This was the full hand:

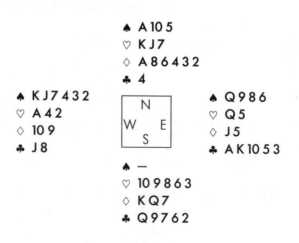

♠ A 10 5
♡ K J 7
◇ A 8 6 4 3 2
♣ 4

♠ K J 7 4 3 2
♡ A 4 2
◇ 10 9
♣ J 8

♠ Q 9 8 6
♡ Q 5
◇ J 5
♣ A K 10 5 3

♠ —
♡ 10 9 8 6 3
◇ K Q 7
♣ Q 9 7 6 2

The East-West par on this deal is Four Spades, against which we can collect 500 on a club lead (or the ace of diamonds and a club switch). Once West had passed as dealer, the tempo of the auction made it tough for the Canadians to realize that they needed to save.

At the other table, our West opens with a weak two in spades and East jumps to game over North's Three Diamonds overcall. It is not at all easy for South to double, and he duly presses on to the hopeless Five Diamonds. So, a game swing to us?

Unfortunately not; East leads a top club and then tries to give his partner a ruff. Declarer puts up dummy's queen and discards his third heart when West follows suit. He subsequently guesses the hearts to score up his contract.

So as it happens, bidding our 19-point game is necessary to avoid losing a double-figure swing. Our plus 620 is worth 1 IMP.

We seem to be making little progress in this stanza and our opponents are doing all of the right things. With the set drawing to a close, RHO deals with just the opponents vulnerable and we pick up:

♠ A K 8 6 ♡ Q 7 4 ◇ 8 ♣ A Q 6 3 2

Baran passes and we unleash our version of the old Precision Two Diamonds opening: **two hearts**, showing 11-15 HCP, at most one diamond and at least 4-3 in the majors.

Eric jumps to **four hearts** and that concludes the brisk auction:

WEST	NORTH	EAST	SOUTH
Molson	Eric	Baran	Us
		pass	2♡
pass	4♡	all pass	

Molson leads the five of hearts and Eric puts down about what I would expect:

♠ 7 5 2
♡ A J 10 9 3 2
♢ Q 7 3
♣ 4

```
      N
   W     E
      S
```

♡ 5 led

♠ A K 8 6
♡ Q 7 4
♢ 8
♣ A Q 6 3 2

It is immediately clear that this is not an ideal hand for our methods. The contract is likely to be the same at the other table, but played from the North seat. Protected from the trump lead, declarer will get home easily by ruffing two diamonds in the South hand — losing just a diamond, a spade and a trump.

It will not help us to refuse the trump finesse (the king might be onside, after all), since if we do, the defenders will probably be able to play a second, and perhaps even a third, trump when we let them in with a diamond. We therefore play low at Trick 1 and East duly wins the king of hearts.

Mark Molson

Surprisingly, Baran now switches to a spade. We will now be able to ruff one diamond at least, but we still need to do something with the clubs. We therefore win the ace of spades, cash the ace of clubs, and ruff a club before playing a diamond from dummy.

East rises with the ace of diamonds and plays a second trump, but we are in control now. We win with the queen of hearts, ruff a club, ruff a diamond, ruff the fourth round of club establishing the long card in the suit, draw the last trump, come to the king of spades, and cash the thirteenth club for ten tricks.

Here is the full deal:

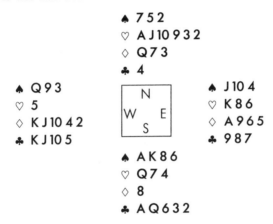

```
                    ♠ 7 5 2
                    ♡ A J 10 9 3 2
                    ◇ Q 7 3
                    ♣ 4
    ♠ Q 9 3          ┌─────────┐      ♠ J 10 4
    ♡ 5              │    N    │      ♡ K 8 6
    ◇ K J 10 4 2     │ W     E │      ◇ A 9 6 5
    ♣ K J 10 5       │    S    │      ♣ 9 8 7
                     └─────────┘
                    ♠ A K 8 6
                    ♡ Q 7 4
                    ◇ 8
                    ♣ A Q 6 3 2
```

It turns out that it is still possible to make the contract if East returns a trump at Trick 2. **Can you see how?**

You must play the ace of clubs, ruff a club and then duck a spade. Suppose that East wins and plays a third trump, you can then win in hand, ruff a club, cross to a high spade, ruff the fourth round of clubs, and then re-enter the South hand to score the long card in both black suits.

Would I have played this way? Perhaps, but then again maybe I would have simply fallen back on the club finesse. Who knows?

Predictably, the Canadians played Four Hearts from the safe side, so this board is flat. Which is more than can be said for the rest of the set — we get trounced 53-12!

With one 16-board stanza to play, our once impressive-looking lead has been reduced to just 26 IMPs.

Of course, we had hoped to put the match beyond reach in the ninth set, but one cannot change the score. Our philosophy is very much 'that's what leads are for'.

Our team is still in good spirits and we try to reassure ourselves by saying that we are 52 IMPs better off than the Canadians (much better to be 25 IMPs ahead than 26 IMPs in arrears). The tension is incredibly high. It does not matter how many times you've been here before. This is what it's all about. It is for this moment that you have practiced for thousands of hours in the course of almost a whole lifetime.

I do not envy the pair from either team who are sitting out the last set. The adrenaline is really flowing — sixteen deals left with the Bermuda Bowl at stake!

Players in the open Vugraph room

Final: Set Ten
Running Score: USA 300 — Canada 274

We return to Vugraph to play the last set of the championships against Kokish-Silver. The stanza starts well at our table and it is quickly apparent that luck is running with us. The opponents know it too — I can see it in their eyes — our 26-IMP lead might as well be 260.

The most interesting board of the set rather sums up the game of bridge. It comes with both the set and the championship drawing to a close. With neither side vulnerable and Eric the dealer, we pick up:

♠ 8732   ♡ A942   ◇ A9   ♣ K86

Eric opens the bidding with a random **one diamond** and we make the obvious **one heart** response. Eric raises to **two hearts** and now we must make a decision. For pairs who favor a style of sound opening bids, a game try would be clear. It is less so for us, as this is not a particularly good hand despite the excellent controls. Nonetheless, we elect to press on with **two notrump** and Eric closes the auction with a jump to **four hearts**.

WEST	NORTH	EAST	SOUTH
Silver	*Eric*	*Kokish*	*Us*
	1◇	pass	1♡
pass	2♡	pass	2NT
pass	4♡	all pass	

Silver leads the five of clubs and Eric produces a hand that most players would not have considered 'an opening bid with extras':

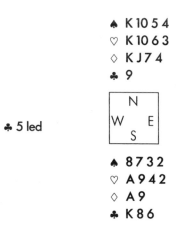

```
          ♠ K 10 5 4
          ♡ K 10 6 3
          ◇ K J 7 4
          ♣ 9
          ┌─────────┐
          │    N    │
  ♣ 5 led │  W   E  │
          │    S    │
          └─────────┘
          ♠ 8 7 3 2
          ♡ A 9 4 2
          ◇ A 9
          ♣ K 8 6
```

East wins the first trick with the ace of clubs and returns the suit. We elect to play low on this trick and ruff in dummy. Then comes the king of hearts and a heart to the nine and West's jack.

West exits with a diamond and we win with the nine, cash the ace of diamonds, and then draw the last trump. It takes East some time to select his discard on the third round of trumps, but he eventually pitches a spade.

When we next lead a spade towards dummy, West hops up with the ace and exits with the jack of spades. We rise with the king and East forlornly follows with the queen. We can now claim an unlikely ten tricks.

Closing Ceremony

At the other table, the Canadian declarer goes one down in the same contract, so we gain 10 IMPs on the deal.

If any of you picked up this book expecting to read about hands on which I made contracts using esoteric squeezes and clever textbook endings, you will still be waiting for such a deal. In reality, even at the World Championship level, most swings occur because someone makes a mistake rather than because of some brilliant play. This final hand rather sums this up. I made the contract because East could not read my distribution, so he made the wrong discard.

As it happens, I missed a textbook play on this deal — one of those that never occur in real life! Can you see what would have happened if I had taken Trick 2 with the king of clubs, discarding a spade from dummy?

I lead a spade next, and suppose West ducks to the king (although it doesn't matter). Now comes the ace of diamonds, a diamond finesse, the king of diamonds and a diamond ruff. I can now ruff a club and exit with a spade to produce the matrix required for a Devil's Coup. (I've executed a grand total of one Devil's Coup in my entire career and, needless to say, it was in a partscore!)

So, there is the perfect textbook hand for which you have been waiting. As you can see, though, it is not such plays that win championships. You win by making fewer errors than your opponents and by capitalizing on their mistakes. To this end, the Meckwell style is to put the opponents under pressure as often as possible. The more decisions you give them, the more they will get wrong and the more chances you will have to take advantage.

We win the final stanza 39-22 and the match by 43 IMPs (339-296). Anyone just looking at the result of the final may think that this was a comfortable win. Having followed our progress throughout this book, you will realize that nothing could be further from the truth.

Having only just managed to survive the Round Robin stage we had to battle through an epic quarter-final and a tough semifinal to meet a Canadian team at the top of their game. Indeed, if one were to ignore the one-sided fifth set of the final, they outscored us over the remaining 148 boards. In fact, they had closed the margin to within 13 IMPs at one point early in the final set.

An easy victory? No. At this level there is no such thing.

The victorious US Team in Beijing, 1995
Hamman, Nickell, Rodwell, Meckstroth, Wolff, Freeman

More Bridge Titles from Master Point Press

Around the World in 80 Hands by Zia Mahmood with David Burn
256pp., PB   Can $22.95   US $16.95

A Study in Silver *A second collection of bridge stories*
by David Silver
128pp., PB   Can $12.95   US$ 9.95

Becoming a Bridge Expert by Frank Stewart
300pp., PB   Can $27.95   US $19.95

Bridge Problems for a New Millenium by Julian Pottage
160pp., PB   Can $14.95   US $14.95

Bridge the Silver Way by David Silver and Tim Bourke
192pp., PB   Can $19.95   US $14.95

Bridge: 25 Ways to Compete in the Bidding.
by Barbara Seagram and Marc Smith
220pp., PB   Can.$19.95   US $15.95

Bridge, Zia... and me by Michael Rosenberg
(foreword by Zia Mahmood)
192pp., PB   Can $19.95   US $15.95

Challenge Your Declarer Play by Danny Roth
128pp., PB   Can. $12.95   US $ 9.95

Classic Kantar a *collection of bridge humor* by Eddie Kantar
192pp., PB   Can $19.95   US$ $14.95

Competitive Bidding in the 21st Century by Marshall Miles
254pp.,PB   Can. $22.95   US. $16.95

Countdown to Winning Bridge by Tim Bourke and Marc Smith
92pp., PB   Can $19.95   US $14.95

Easier Done Than Said *Brilliancy at the Bridge Table*
by Prakash K. Paranjape
128pp., PB   Can $15.95   US $12.95

For Love or Money *The Life of a Bridge Journalist*
by Mark Horton and Brian Senior
189pp., PB   Can $22.95   US $16.95

Focus On Declarer Play by Danny Roth
128pp., PB   Can $12.95   US $9.95

Focus On Defence by Danny Roth
128pp., PB   Can $12.95   US $9.95

Focus On Bidding by Danny Roth
160pp., PB   Can $14.95   US $11.95

I Shot my Bridge Partner by Matthew Granovetter
384pp., PB   Can $19.95   US $14.95

Murder at the Bridge Table by Matthew Granovetter
320pp., PB   Can $19.95   US $14.95

Partnership Bidding a workbook by Mary Paul
96pp., PB   Can $9.95   US $7.95
Playing with the Bridge Legends by Barnet Shenkin
(forewords by Zia and Michael Rosenberg)
240pp., PB   Can $24.95   US $17.95

Saints and Sinners *The St. Titus Bridge Challenge*
by David Bird & Tim Bourke
192pp., PB   Can $19.95   US $14.95

Samurai Bridge *A tale of old Japan* by Robert F. MacKinnon
256pp., PB   Can $ 22.95   US $16.95

Tales out of School *'Bridge 101' and other stories* by David Silver
(foreword by Dorothy Hayden Truscott)
128pp., PB   Can $ 12.95   US $9.95

The Bridge Magicians by Mark Horton and Radoslaw Kielbasinski
248pp., PB   Can $24.95   US $17.95

The Bridge Player's Bedside Book edited by Tony Forrester
256pp., HC   Can $27.95   US $19.95

The Complete Book of BOLS Bridge Tips edited by Sally Brock
176pp., PB (photographs)   Can $24.95   US$17.95

There Must Be A Way... *52 challenging bridge hands*
by Andrew Diosy (foreword by Eddie Kantar)
96pp., PB $9.95 US & Can.

You Have to See This... *52 more challenging bridge problems*
by Andrew Diosy and Linda Lee
96pp., PB   Can $12.95   US $9.95

World Class — *conversations with the bridge masters* by Marc Smith
288pp., PB (photographs)   Can $24.95   US $17.95